LIGHT FROM BEYOND THE TOMB

Spiritualism Survived

MARILYN J. AWTRY

LIGHT FROM BEYOND THE TOMB

Spiritualism Survived

MARILYN J. AWTRY

Author of "RIVER OF LIFE – How to Live in the Flow

Copyright © 2010 Marilyn J. Awtry

Published by:
Shen-men Publishing
Sanford, FL
www.shenmenpublishing.com
Phone: 407-322-7585

Book Formatting and cover design by: Kimberly Martin

All rights reserved. No part of this book may be reproduced in any manner whatsoever without written permission from the author, except in the case of brief quotations embodied in critical articles, reviews and books with suitable credits.

First Published by
Shen-men Publishing
July 1, 2010

ISBN 978-0-615-37020-0
Library of Congress Control Number: 2010905684

Printed in the United States of America

This Book
is
Dedicated to
The Memory Of

The Peddler
CHARLES B. ROSNA

~ ~ ~

The Organizer
ANNA LEAH FOX UNDERHILL

~ ~ ~

The Mediums
MARGARETTA (MAGGIE) FOX KANE
CATHERINE (KATIE) FOX JENCKEN

Acknowledgments

The author would like to express her deepest appreciation to the following for their invaluable assistance in the creation of this book.

First would be my thanks to those in Spirit who tried in every way to bring my attention to the book written by Reuben B. Davenport and the need to let the world know <u>The Death-Blow to Spiritualism</u> was ineffective.

My deepest appreciation to a dedicated student of Modern Spiritualism—Kerri Hartman—for carefully reading the manuscript and asking questions that alerted me of the need for clarity to have the book appeal to the newcomer as well as the long time Spiritualists.

Table of Contents

Introduction i
Preface v

I   It All Started Here 1
II   The News Spreads 13
III   Elisha Kent Kane's Love 23
IV   The Spiritual Mansion 29
V   God Has Not Ordered It 33
VI   The Discomforted Enemy 41
VII   The Second Blow 47
VIII "The Recantation" 55
IX   Life Goes On 69
X   Light From Beyond The Tomb 75
XI   Fact & Fiction 93
XII   Spiritualism's Stepping Stones - A Review 101
XIII Conclusion 109

Appendix A - Participants 115
Appendix B - Directions to Hydesville Memorial Park 117
Reference Material 119
About the Author 121
Author's Publications 122

Introduction

The Death-Blow to Spiritualism was written by Reuben Briggs Davenport in 1888. In the Introduction, he states that a "*bold fabric of lies built up to sustain the claim that the 'rappings' in which all spiritualistic so-called phenomena originated were unaccountable except on the supernatural hypothesis, can no longer be cited to an intelligent mind. The elaborate narrative* entitled The Missing Link in Modern Spiritualism *published by the eldest sister Mrs. Ann (sic) Leah (Fish) Fox Underhill, who is now the only remaining stay of spiritualistic deception, is proved to be false from title page to finish.*" The question we ask today is, "Can you prove it now, Mr. Davenport?"

Davenport goes on to elaborate that the Fox Sisters at that time (1888) "*are now most earnest in denunciation of those impostures; the most eager to dissipate the foolish belief of thousands in the flimsiest system of deception that was ever cloaked with the hypocrisy of a so-called religion.*" Would you think so now, Mr. Davenport?

He tells how "*when, by accident, they discovered a method of deceiving those around them by means of mysterious noises, they were but little children, innocent of the thought of wrong, ignorant of the world and the world's guile, and imagining only that what they did was a clever lark, such as the adult age easily pardons to exuberant and spritely youth.*"

Davenport went on to elaborate by saying the "*two children, who, had at first delighted, as younglings will, in what was but a laughable mystification, were dragged into a sordid, wicked and loathsome speculation, built upon lying and fraud, as unforgivable as the sin of Satan, and of which they were but the unthinking instruments, often reluctant and remorseful, yet docile and compliant by nature."*

Davenport further states: *"From this came the 'Rochester knockings' as an example and prototype of all so-called spiritualist phenomena. These two young children were carried away by the undreamt of current of enthusiasm and in awe of it all."*

Davenport tells how the children traveled from stage-to-stage to repeat their part over and over again. Their belief in communication with the spirits of the departed was misguided. He goes on to say *"from such slight and trivial beginning came the great movement—great because of the number which it comprised and of the sensation which attended its progress—that for more than forty years has alternately surprised, puzzled, disgusted and amused the world."* By his own expression, it becomes apparent that he was in with the group who were against the phenomena and the new movement that had been named "Modern Spiritualism."

He once again reminds us that the young girls were dragged into this life as young children. However, they were *"rescued from it for an interval by two men whose names are historical, (Dr. Kane & Horace Greeley) the one as a hero and explorer, and the other as a journalist and daily philosopher; borne back to it again by the tide of ill-fortune; used and controlled, by those whose hearts were 'dry as summer's dust,' for their own hateful purposes; menaced when conscience rebelled and suggested retraction and amends... .—Margaretta and Catherine Fox now denounce and anathematize Spiritualism as absolutely and utterly false from beginning to end; and they declare their solemn intention to devote themselves henceforth to the noble task of undoing the great evil which they have done... ."*

He goes on to say that in the pages that would follow, he would give the "real" story of the lives of Mrs. Kane and Mrs. Jencken as it aligns to Spiritualism. And so that is the story Davenport told and the one that he apparently so desperately wanted us all to believe.

However, what may or may not have been true in 1888 definitely was proven **not** to be truth less than a year later in November 1889. The story told in 1888 certainly was totally unraveled by the facts of 1889, as well as the major incident that took place in Hydesville in 1904.

It is my intention to provide the complete story which will conclude that the Davenport's death-blow "failed." I will follow the Chapters of <u>The Death-Blow to Spiritualism</u> as closely as possible and conclude with the facts that actually "killed the death-blow itself."

Spiritualism is alive and well in the 21st Century.

Marilyn J. Awtry
July 2010

Preface

It has often been said that "time changes all things." This story written herein is proof positive that the statement is a fact in regard to Spiritualism. In 1888, a book was written by Reuben Briggs Davenport. It was entitled <u>The Death-Blow to Spiritualism Being the True Story of the Fox Sisters as revealed by Authority of Margaret Fox Kane and Catherine Fox Jencken.</u> He said that the book was the true story of the Fox Sisters as revealed by the authority of Margaret (sic) Fox Kane and Catherine Fox Jencken. However, his truth of the times was all short-lived.

At the time the book was released, the Preface contained the following statement:

"This book has been written in extreme haste. It does not pretend to literary style. But it pretends to absolute truthfulness and a reverent regard for justice. Its sole value, is its character as a contribution to the real history of Spiritualism. As such, it is unquestionably of great importance, greater even than any work of the kind that has been published since the beginning of Modern Spiritualism."

The fly sheet of his book shows the statement made and signed by both of the Fox sisters in 1888. It is as follows:

> "We hereby approve of Mr. Reuben B. Davenport's design to write a true account of the origin of Spiritualism and of our connection therewith, and we authorize him to make proper use of all data that we furnish him."
>
> New York 15th Oct., 1888.
> /s/ Margaret Fox Kane
> /s/ Catherine Fox Jencken

Since the Preface stated that the book had been written in extreme haste and that it did not pretend to be literary style, the question now asked is "What was the hurry?" It was well known at that time that Davenport was not a supporter of the new movement. He had stated that the book was greater than any work of its kind that had been published since the beginning of Modern Spiritualism. And, in fact he thought it was just what the title suggested—"The Death-Blow to Spiritualism."

Was he correct?

I

It All Started Here
1510 Hydesville Road, Hydesville, NY

The Story

A brief of the happenings in the spring of 1848 are offered here for any who may not have heard the story. It is always good to know the humble beginnings before following the long saga of events that took place in the birth of Modern Spiritualism on March 31, 1848 and the lives of the Fox Sisters: Leah, Maggie and Katie. Although Leah made her transition to the World of Spirit in 1890, Catherine (Katie) in 1892, and Margaretta (Maggie) following in 1893, many variations of the story continue to be written today.

The major event of 1848 as well as the lives of the sisters have been told many times and I dare say in various convincing versions; however, while most contained facts, many did not lack in fiction. It is noted that the happenings of 1848 were recorded in that same year by E. E. Lewis and entitled *"A Report of the Mysterious Noises Heard in the House of Mr. John D. Fox in Hydesville, Arcadia, Wayne County; authenticated by the Certificates and confirmed by the Statements of the Citizens of that Place and Vicinity."* Therefore, it might be assumed it would be more accurate than other accounts written in later years or others that had been copied from yet another version. In searching through the many documents, it was found that some written at a later date had the original certificates or copies; however, some of the copies had been altered.

The Beginning

It was in the little hamlet of Hydesville in Acadia Township, near Newark in Wayne County, New York, that the Science, Philosophy, and Religion of Modern Spiritualism had its humble beginning. In 1810, the hamlet was actually named Hydeville after Dr. Henry Hyde. It was in the town of Sodus, Ontario County. In 1811, part of the area was set off as the town of Lyons. In 1823, Wayne County was established. The forming of the township of Arcadia came in 1825.

Dr. Henry Hyde had constructed a cottage here with the intention of practicing medicine. He obviously had not searched out the conditions in the community before taking on the idea of constructing a home and a medical practice. Or perhaps he had searched and found that the Erie Canal (1817) was proposed to flow just a few feet from the main road. That, no doubt in itself, would have created an excellent flow of business. But, because of lack of foresight, the townspeople cried out loudly and prevented the canal from being constructed there. Of course, this later proved to be a very poor judgment by the community. After the canal was constructed in another area, it gave birth to the affluent settlements of Newark and Arcadia/Lockville.

The cottage was finally completed and Dr. Henry Hyde settled in. A short time after moving into his house, Dr. Hyde found that due to the sparsely settled community and the financial condition of its inhabitants, a medical practice would not provide a lucrative income. Like any other good business person, it was time to regroup. Now that he had lived in the hamlet for a reasonable period of time, he had the opportunity to become familiar with the area. This gave birth to another idea. Dr. Henry Hyde built and operated a tavern just across from the corner of Hydeville and Parker Roads. This endeavor proved to be very successful as it filled the needs of his fellow pioneers. The tavern also became a regular stop-off for persons traveling westward.

Once again, we find various stories about Hydeville at that period of time. For instance, it had been a farming community with a church, school house, tavern, blacksmith shop, grist mills, and hat manufacturing plant as well as a variety of other small businesses that have faded with the past. The most controversial issue about that timeframe was the total of inhabitants in the hamlet. Some have stated it to have had at least 500 inhabitants. If that were true, it should have been able to support a local doctor. The three facts that can be told today and supported by their remains are the building that housed the Methodist church that stands in a grassy plot next to Dr. Hyde's property, the old two-story brick school house at the fork of Parker Road just two miles down from the cottage, and the original foundation of the cottage that Dr. Hyde had constructed on the corner at 1510

Hydesville Road. Later, that cottage was to become known as "The Fox Cottage." Time brings change and is reflected here in that all of the other buildings in the community have faded away with the past.

Dr. Henry Hyde passed to Spirit in 1828. Eventually his son, Artemas W. Hyde, continued in his father's footsteps of becoming a wealthy man. However, he did it differently. Artemas became the owner of very large parcels of land. Records show that he became known as having the most valuable farm-holdings in all of Arcadia.

Fox Family Brief

John David Fox descended from immigrants who came from the Palatine section of Germany and settled in New City, Rockland County, New York. This is just northwest of the Hudson River and New York City. John was a blacksmith. Margaret Rutan Smith came from Canada to New City to visit relatives and then stayed on for some time. She was of Dutch, English and French descent. Her grandmother, Margaret Rutan Ackerman was known to have an affinity for the occult. Her sister Elizabeth predicted many future events including the date of her own death. In 1812, Margaret married John D. Fox.

In New City, (often erroneously recorded in many books and articles as New York City) John and Margaret became the proud parents of Emily in 1813, Anna Leah in 1814, Maria Adalea in 1816, Elizabeth in 1818, and David Stephen in 1820. As time passed, it became evident that all was not well within the family. Due to Mr. Fox's drinking habits, the family became divided. Mrs. Fox moved her family back to be with relatives in Consecon, Canada, on Lake Ontario. More years passed and time brought a reformation of Mr. Fox's habit and thus set the stage for the reuniting of the family in Canada. This resulted in the birth of Margaretta in Fall of 1837, and Catherine in the Spring of 1839.

Leah, the oldest living daughter, had married at the age of fourteen and five months to Bowman Fish, a man her elder by several years. They lived in Rochester, New York. In 1830, they had one daughter whom they named Elizabeth, later to become known as Lizzie (not to be confused with David's daughter born several years later). After a few years of marriage, Fish realized that Leah was but a child herself. Much to her surprise, he deserted her and their daughter. The story told, whether fact or fiction, is that he went west and married a wealthy woman. After leaving Leah and Lizzie, no record of him has been found. However, it should be known that during their marriage, he did provide a comfortable home for the family. He also made provisions for Leah to take music lessons. She became a very proficient pianist. This indeed became an asset for her. Because of this talent, Leah was able to provide a living for herself and her daughter by giving piano lessons. She was quite popular as a music teacher and had a full register of students.

Time fleeted by and after Margaret and John reunited, the Fox family moved from Canada back to New City in Rockland County. A short time thereafter, the Fox family moved to Rochester and lived with Leah for several months. John and Margaret's son David, once a blacksmith, was now a farmer in Hydesville. He lived on Parker Road just two miles from the Hyde cottage in the house constructed by his uncle, John Smith (Margaret's brother). John Fox planned to build a house for his family on David's property as well as a blacksmith shop. However, the winter weather was a negative factor and the beginning of construction was postponed until the spring of 1848. In order to have his family come from Rochester to be with him, he rented Dr. Henry Hyde's cottage at 1510 Hydesville Road on the corner of Parker Road.

The Cottage Tenants & That Notorious Event

During 1843-1844, the cottage had been rented by the Bell family. Little is known of that residency except that they were well-liked in the neighborhood and they had a local young lady by the name of Lucretia Pulver doing housework and cooking for them. In order for her to attend school, she often stayed with the Bells. It is also known that the Bell's neighborhood had the services of an itinerant peddler from Orleans County, N.Y.

The next tenants of the cottage from 1846-1847 were Michael Weekman, his wife, and two young daughters. They had been disturbed by the uncanny noises that vibrated from various areas of the house. Their servant, Mrs. Lape, saw a gentleman standing in the room but by the time her call for help was answered, he had simply faded away. Another time that disturbances occurred, Mrs. Weekman testified:

> "We heard great noises during the night; sometimes a sound as if a person was walking in the cellar. One night, one of our little girls, who slept in the room where the noises were heard, awoke us all up by her screaming very loudly. My husband and myself and our hired girl all went to the room to see what was the matter with her. The child sat up in bed, crying and screaming, and it was some time before we could quiet her enough to get answers to our questions. She said something had been moving around her and over her head and face; that it was cold, and that she felt it all over her... . We took her into bed with us, and it was a long time before we could get her to sleep in that bed again."

Although the Weekmans had withstood the various noises, once their youngest daughter was scared to hysteria by the noises and other happenings—enough was enough! The Weekman family packed up and moved out of the cottage. The disturbances remained for the Fox family to address.

On the blustery cold winter day of Saturday, December 11, 1847, John David Fox and his wife, Margaret Smith Fox, along with their two youngest children Margaretta (Maggie), age 11 and Catherine (Katie), age nine, moved into the cottage at 1510 Hydesville Road. Their closest living relative was David Stephen Fox and his wife Elizabeth Culver Fox and their children. They lived on Parker Road, exactly two miles from the corner of Hydesville and Parker Road where the Fox cottage stood. Although it was a temporary move, Margaret Fox set out to make it a comfortable place for the family to abide. The John Fox family enjoyed the cottage and was extremely thrilled to be living close to David and his family. They settled in and lived happily—until.

During the first three months of their tenancy in the cottage, any noise that might have been heard was of no consequence. According to Mrs. Fox, the noises built up and became prominent about March 15th. At that time, the noises became a nightly disturbance interrupting their sleep. However, they continued to try to ignore it but to no avail. The noises continued to be extremely disturbing and at times, they only took place when the two young children were awake. Some of the time, it sounded as if furniture was being moved around the room; at other times the shuffling of feet. However after every inspection, everything was always found to be in place. The lack of sleep caused by the ever recurring noises brought a heavy weariness upon the family. Mrs. Fox testified that the noises at times sounded like someone knocking on the floor in what was called the east bedroom or sounded as if a chair moved across the floor.

Finally on Friday, March 31, 1848, their exhaustion forced the family to retire early. The children were tucked in their bed in the east room and the parents in the adjoining chamber. Sleep was not to come! Both Mr. & Mrs. Fox had searched the house many times before in an attempt to discover the cause of the rapping, stomping, and shuffling sounds. Every night the noises became more and more disturbing. On this night, the children lay side-by-side listening attentively to the incessant rappings. Finally, they tried to make similar sounds. Katie began snapping her fingers and the same sound immediately responded. When she stopped, the responding sound stopped. Then, Maggie joined in by saying in sport, "Now, do just as I do" and she counted "one, two, three and four" striking one hand in the other at the same time. The response was exactly the same number of raps.

In previous years, several members of Mrs. Fox's family demonstrated mediumship. She had repeatedly attended séances held by her family members and she knew exactly what steps should be taken now. Supposing the sounds to be that of a Spirit entity, Mrs. Fox proceeded by asking the "noise" to "count ten" and the response was an immediate ten raps. She then asked questions in an attempt to identify the Spirit. Mrs. Fox asked, "Is this a human being that answers my questions correctly?" There was silence. Then she asked, "Is it a Spirit? If so, make two raps." Immediately two raps were heard. Mrs. Fox then queried: "Is this an injured Spirit, make two raps?" Instantly, two raps caused the house to tremble. Next, Mrs. Fox asked: "Were you injured in this house?" Since the question had been partially answered previously, she asked specifically: "Is the person living that injured you?" Raps were heard again. Mrs. Fox thought that it might be wise to put the Spirit to a test by asking the ages of her children. Successively, the raps correctly identified each child's age. Although only six children were alive, there were seven raps. After the seventh rap, there was a slight pause that was followed by three more emphatic raps. That was the age of their daughter Emily born in 1813 who passed on in her infancy. Although the Fox family lived in New City at that time, it is said by some but not confirmed that they interred little Emily near David's property in Hydesville.

As the questioning continued, Mrs. Fox ascertained that the Spirit was that of a 31 year old man. His answers to the questions revealed he had been murdered in the house for the sum of $500. Continuing the conversation, she learned his remains were buried in the cellar of the house. The Spirit also clarified that he had a wife and five children—two sons and three daughters—and that they were all living at the time of his murder. However, his wife had since passed on.

Mrs. Fox then asked if the Spirit would rap if she invited neighbors in to witness the phenomenon. The answer was in the affirmative. Mr. Fox immediately invited the neighbors in for a session. Being most anxiousness to partake of the happenings and to witness the unexplainable phenomenon, their neighbors, Mr. & Mrs. Redfield came first and then others followed. The Spirit answered all of Mrs. Redfield's questions accurately. After this time, the neighbors gathered regularly at the house to ask questions and hear the continuing raps. More questions and the responsive rappings created an unexplainable stir that awakened the neighborhood that was once a quiet, sleepy hamlet. Mr. and Mrs. Fox, as well as some of the neighbors, then signed affidavits attesting to the fact that the events in the house on the corner of Parker Road and Hydesville Road in the hamlet of Hydesville were true.

The night after the first séance, Mrs. Fox stayed in Mrs. Redfield's home. The girls stayed with other neighbors. Mr. Redfield and Mr. Fox stayed in the cottage. For days, people continued to come to check out the unusual happenings in the cottage. As the word spread further of the goings on in Hydesville, more crowds came from near and far to view the so-called "haunted house" and perhaps hear the rappings. The numbers were compounded as the neighborhood men gathered to discuss digging in the cellar in an attempt to locate the buried body. They finally appointed a committee to ask questions again. Once again, they were well satisfied with the answers provided by raps. On Sunday morning, April 2nd, the noise was quite loud and they commenced digging in the cellar of the cottage; however, the flood waters came and they were forced to give up. Mud Creek ran down the side of the property and was known to flood in the spring time. All of this commotion made it obvious that the Fox family must move to other quarters. They just could not go back to live in the house. So the Fox family temporarily moved in with David and his family just two miles down the bumpy, sandy, and dirt-laden Parker Road. However, the rappings followed them. They did not stop!

II
The News Spreads

The Initial Excitement

To some degree, the initial excitement subsided somewhat in Hydesville. However, the news that had once caused great excitement in the hamlet was now in pamphlet form put out by the press detailing the whole uncanny and odd happenings in the cottage at Hydesville. This news raised excitement in several counties. By early May 1848, after being asked many questions that would identify her family, Leah, in Rochester, was handed a copy of the pamphlet. She was astounded at the report; however, she affirmed that if her family signed the affidavits documenting the happenings, she knew it was true.

Leah Makes Her Mark

Leah immediately packed her luggage. She and her 18 year old daughter Elizabeth (Lizzie) traveled the first night packet boat (mail boat) to Newark via the Erie Canal. Once they located the stables near the dock, they continued traveling to Hydesville by horse and carriage. On arrival, they found the cottage standing bare and alone. The family was not there. The driver informed her that her parents and sisters had left the cottage and moved into David's house.

Leah directed the driver to go directly there. Shortly after their arrival at David's house, it became apparent that the raps and noises had moved with the Fox family.

After two weeks of little peace and much discussion, it was decided that perhaps if the two young children were separated the noises would cease. Leah wanted to take Katie with her to Rochester since she had started the communication with the Spirit entity. However, Mr. Fox felt that at nine years old, she was far too young to leave home. After much discussion and persuasion by Leah, Mr. Fox agreed that Maggie could go to Rochester with Leah. In haste, Leah packed up Maggie and Lizzie and traveled back to Rochester by boat via the Erie Canal. However, it quickly became apparent that this move was not successful in stopping the raps. Much to their surprise, bold and loud raps were heard at the dinner table in the cabin of the boat.

Once Leah, Lizzie & Maggie were settled back in Rochester, the manifestations only became more emphatic. Leah's home adjoined a graveyard and she believed it was instrumental in the manifestations doubling. The next step was to move away from the graveyard. Leah rented a house a short distance away on Troup Street. That did not end the noises either. Leah decided it best not to try to ignore the raps any longer. She commenced holding séances in her home and inviting those she felt would be supportive of her and the communication with the unseen. One of the couples, Isaac and Amy Post, were radical Hicksite Quakers involved in many of the issues of the day, such as women's rights and abolitionism. They became some of the first believers in Spiritualism. Leah had a wide variety of friends, so she decided to invite small groups at a time into her home for séances. However, Maggie became despondent being away from her beloved sister Katie. So Leah in her convincing manner pleaded with Mama Fox to bring Katie to Rochester. Mrs. Fox fell into Leah's well planned trap and Mrs. Fox and Katie went to stay with her, Lizzie and Maggie. Once they had settled in, Leah invited a group of friends to join them for a séance. The meetings continued and one of the most important messages from the Spirits was this: "*Dear Friends, you must proclaim these truths to the world. This is the dawning of a new era; and you must not try to conceal it any longer. When you do your duty, God will protect you and good Spirits will watch over you.*" Leah was determined to build the new religion she had dreamed of having for a long time. Perhaps now, it happened; Modern Spiritualism had been born!

First Stop: Rochester

Word of the three Fox sisters residing in Rochester soon became common knowledge. Séances occurred several times a week. The Committee of faithful friends always required some reliable person be present. They were very protective of the Fox family. They did everything possible to protect them. One of the prominent committees consisted of well-known men in various professions such as Isaac Post, R. D. Jones, Edward Jones, John Kedzie and Andrew Crackner. After many séances at Leah's home, the message from the Spirit world was adamant in having a public demonstration of the rappings. After much discussion and planning, on Wednesday, November 14, 1849, the first public demonstration was held at Corinthian Hall in Rochester, New York. Maggie and Katie were brought to the stage only after being carefully examined by a group of women to assure they had no tricks up their sleeves.

In Reuben B. Davenport's book, he takes a dim view of Leah. He clearly makes the point that Leah saw nothing but fame and money as a result of her sisters' mediumship. Others saw her as almost saint-like and a protective older sister. Yet others wondered if she was a demanding, manipulative person willing to sacrifice the happiness and welfare of her younger sisters for fame and prosperity that the new Spiritualist movement brought to the family. Each had their own opinion of Leah. The next step that didn't sit well with many was the instituting of fees for the services of the young mediums. But it must be known that this was not the idea of the Fox family; however, for good reason, it was suggested by the committee.

Time passed and the Fox sisters made their debut in various parts of New York State and became well known in New York City, Ohio, Pennsylvania, Massachusetts, Washington, D.C., and elsewhere. In 1850, they were welcomed in New York City by the famed Horace Greeley, American newspaper owner and editor, founder of the Liberal Republican Party, a reformer, and a politician. His <u>New York Tribune</u> was America's most influential newspaper from the 1840s through the 1870s. Many considered him the greatest editor of his day. Greeley graciously opened his stylish home to the Fox family and became a staunch protector of them. Noting Katie's young age, he immediately made it clear she must be placed in school. Having no objection from her mother, he took the necessary steps and Katie's education began. While in the city, the girls demonstrated mediumship at home séances as well as in public meetings. Their lives had now changed forever. Because of a very demanding public, they had little time for themselves.

Investigation of the girls and the phenomena produced in their presence was scrutinized by the well known of the day. Most of the assumptions made were negative. Horace Greeley was distressed by the negative remarks concerning the girls and he published the following article in the New York Tribune:

THE MYSTERIOUS HAPPENINGS

"Mrs. Fox and her three daughters left our city yesterday on their return to Rochester, after a stay here of some weeks; during which they have subjected the mysterious influence by which they seem to be accompanied, to every reasonable test and to the keen and critical scrutiny of hundreds who have chosen to visit them or whom they have been invited to visit. The rooms which they occupied have been repeatedly searched and scrutinized; they have been taken without an hour's notice to houses they had never before entered; they have been all unconsciously placed on a glass surface, concealed under the carpet, in order to interrupt electrical vibrations; they have been disrobed by a committee of ladies, appointed without notice and insisting that neither of them should leave the room until the investigation had been made, etc. etc; yet we believe no one, to this moment, pretends that he has detected either of them producing or causing the 'rapping's,' (sic) nor do we think any of their contemners has invented plausible theory to account for the production of these sounds, nor the singular intelligence which seemed certainly at times has seemed to be manifest through them.

Some ten or twelve days since they gave up their rooms at the hotel, and devoted the remainder of their sojourn here to visiting several families, to which they had been invited by persons interested in the subject, and subjecting the singular influence to a closer, calmer examination than could be given to it at a hotel, and before casual companies of strangers, drawn together by vague curiosity more than rational interest, or predetermined and invincible hostility. Our own dwelling was among those they visited; not only submitting to, but courting, the fullest and keenest inquiry with regard to the alleged manifestations from the Spirit world, by which they were attended. We devoted what time we could spare from our duties, out of three days, to this subject. It would be the basest cowardice not to say that we are convinced beyond a doubt, of their perfect integrity and good faith while on the premises. Whatever may be the origin or cause of the rapping's, (sic) the ladies in whose presence they occurred did not make them. We tested this thoroughly and to our entire satisfaction."

The News Spreads

Six years after the movement began in 1848, mediums sprouted up every where under the tutelage of the Fox sisters. However, this did not stop the questioning of the "how and why" of the phenomena. In 1854, it was discussed that there should be an investigation made to study the phenomena of Spiritualism. This resulted in a petition being sent to Congress asking that a committee be appointed to conduct a scientific investigation of the phenomena of Spiritualism. It was felt that if the first signature on the petition was someone of stature, more attention would be given to the request. Thus, Senator James Shields of Illinois sought out Nathaniel P. Tallmadge who had served as a Senator in New York and Governor of the Wisconsin Territory. He was approached and agreed to be the lead name on the petition. The petition bore his signature on the top of the list of 12,000 signatures. Senator J. Shields presented the petition to Congress on Friday, April 14, 1854. For a historical record, Senator Shields, in a rather skillful, contemporaneous characterization of the matter, said:

"I beg leave to present to the Senate a petition, with some 15,000 (actually 12 thousand after any duplicates were removed, along with signatures that were not legible) names appended to it, upon a very singular and novel subject. The petitioners declare that certain physical and mental phenomena of mysterious import have become so prevalent in this country and Europe, as to engross a large share of public attention.

A partial analysis of these phenomena attests the existence,

"First, of an occult force which is exhibited in sliding, raising, arresting, holding, suspending, and otherwise disturbing ponderable bodies, apparently in direct opposition to the acknowledged laws of matter, and transcending the accredited power of the human mind.

Secondly, lights of different degrees of intensity appear in dark rooms, where chemical action or phosphorescent illumination cannot be developed, and where there are no means of generating electricity or of production combustion.

Thirdly, a variety of sounds, frequent in occurrence, and diversified in character, and of singular significance and importance, consisting of mysterious rappings, indicates the presence of an invisible intelligence.

Sounds are often heard like those produced by the prosecution of mechanical operations, like the hoarse murmur of the winds and waves, mingled with the harsh creaking of the masts and rigging of a ship laboring in a sea. Concussions also occur, resembling distant thunder, producing oscillatory movements of surrounding objects and a tremulous motion of the premises upon which these phenomena occur. Harmonious sounds, as those of human voices, and other sounds resembling those of the fife, drum, trumpet, etc. have been produced without any visible agency.

Fourthly, all the functions of the human body and mind are influenced in what appear to be certain abnormal states of the system, by causes not yet adequately understood or accounted for. The occult force, or invisible power, frequently interrupts the normal operations of the faculties, suspending sensation and voluntary motion of the body to a death-like coldness and rigidity, and diseases hitherto considered incurable, have been entirely eradicated by this mysterious agency.

The petitioners proceed to state that two opinions prevail with respect to the origin of these phenomena. One ascribes them to the power and intelligence of departed Spirits operating under the elements which pervade all natural forms. The other rejects this conclusion, and contends that all these results may be accounted for in a rational and satisfactory manner.

The memorialist, while thus disagreeing as to the cause, concur in the opinion as to the occurrence of the 'alleged phenomena' and in view of their origin, nature and bearing upon the interests of mankind, demand for them a patient, rigid, scientific investigation, and request the appointment of a scientific commission for that purpose.

I have now given a faithful synopsis of this petition, which, however unprecedented in itself, has been prepared with singular ability, presenting the subject with great delicacy and moderation. I make it a rule to present any petition to the Senate, which is respectful in terms; but having discharged this duty, I may be permitted to say that the prevalence of this delusion at this age of the world, among any considerable portion of our citizens, must originate in my opinion, in a defective system of education, or in a partial derangement of

> *the mental faculties, produced by a diseased condition of the physical organization.*
>
> *I cannot, therefore believe that it prevails to the extent indicated in this petition... ."*

A lengthy debate followed. Mr. Petit proposed to refer the petition of the Spiritualists to 3,000 clergymen. Mr. Weller proposed to refer it to the Committee on Foreign Relations, as it might be necessary to inquire whether or not when Americans leave this world they lose their citizenship. Mr. Mason proposed that it should be left to the Committee of Military affairs. Senator Shields himself said he thought of proposing to refer the petition to the Committee on Post Offices and Post Roads because there may be a possibility of establishing a spiritual telegraph between the material and spiritual world. After a prolonged debate, the petition was finally, by a decisive vote, laid upon the table.

III
Elisha Kent Kane's Love

Dr. Elisha Kent Kane

Dr. Elisha Kane, the famous Arctic Explorer, was now 32 years of age. He began his career as a medical doctor in the Navy. After many sojourns, in 1850 he was appointed to his first Arctic exploration in search of the missing Sir John Franklin, a British naval officer and Arctic explorer. Franklin disappeared in an attempt to chart the Northwest Passage in North America and the Arctic. Although they found Franklin's winter camp, they never located the man himself. Kane made his second trip in 1853 constantly bearing northward, finally reaching the North Pole. Kane's Arctic explorations brought him fame and glory. He was awarded medals of honor as well as having a destroyer vessel named in his honor—the USS Kane. Honor upon honor was granted to him.

Although Kane had many successes, received many medals, had vessels named in his honor, and headlines in the news from time to time, his happiness was blurred. Kane deeply mourned the death of his 14 year old brother Willie who passed in 1852.

Kane Is Snared

Although Kane's heart had never been touched, he succumbed to the sweet charm of an attractive young lady. Kane first saw Maggie Fox in the autumn of 1852 at the Webb Union Hotel in Philadelphia, when she was a young lady just turning 15 years of age. Mrs. Fox and Maggie had registered in this noted hotel in order to provide an attractive parlor where Maggie could engage in her Spiritualistic manifestations.

Once Kane's eyes fell on Maggie's beauty, she remained forever in his heart and all too often on his mind. His interest in her was pure and elevated but "it led him to gloomy apprehensions of the fate of so fair, yet so misguided, a creature." He found any plausible reason to visit the hotel parlor often. After frequent visits of pursuing Maggie, he finally won her love. He wrote many a note begging her to give up this life. He often wrote to her in verse and once wrote a prophecy that she would "live and die forlorn."

Kane wrote that *"Maggie was a strange mixture of child and woman, of simplicity and cunning, of passionate impulse and extreme self-control that made her a curious study."* He took a very personal interest in her since just the thought of her was buried deeply within his heart. One of Maggie's friends described that period of time saying:

> *"Little as she (Margaretta) suspected his feelings, he loved her at first sight. Her beauty was that delicate kind which grows on the heart, rather than captivates*

the sense at a glance; she possessed in a high degree that retiring modesty which shuns rather than seeks admiration. The position in which she was placed imposed on her unusual reserve and self control… . To appreciate her real superiority, her age and the circumstances must be considered. She was yet a little child, untutored, except in the elements of instruction to be gained in country district schools, when it was discovered that she possessed a mysterious power, for which no science or theory could account. This brought her at once into notoriety, and gathered around her those who had a fancy for the supernatural, and who loved to excite the wonder of strangers. Most little girls would have been spoiled by that kind of attention."

From the beginning of December 1852, Kane wrote her a daily note. He begged her time and time again to give up the rappings for they would lead her "no where." In January 1853, he wrote reminding her "that she was fitted by nature for better things, and that she would, if she persisted in following the life of a medium, deny herself the highest destiny of a woman." His next step was to discuss Margaretta's need for an education. Finally in early May of 1853, with Leah's furious objection yet with her mother's approval, Maggie moved to Pennsylvania, to study at Mrs. Turner's School in Crookville and be under the charge of Kane's aunt, Mrs. Leiper. There, with an aching heart, Kane left her as he returned to his explorations. During that same time, Maggie studied and made an attempt at pleasing Kane but she became unhappy and despondent. At one point, she became extremely ill and was taken home to her mother and sisters to recuperate and restore her mind to a balance.

On Kane's return from the sea on October 11, 1855, he desperately tried to get his family and friends to accept Maggie. Although, he knew it a difficult thing to accomplish, he did not give up trying. But, he failed—it just would not happen. Much to Kane's dismay, in 1856 Maggie returned to her old association of Spiritualist circles. In order to provide an adequate reading parlor and séance room for the girls, Mrs. Fox rented a larger house on East 22nd Street in New York City.

Dr. Kane was 17 years senior to Maggie who was now just over 18. He was preparing his return to the seas and felt it time to convince Mrs. Fox of his love for Maggie. On the night before his departure in August 1856, in the presence of Mrs. Fox and Katie, Dr. Elisha K. Kane and Maggie were married at E. 22nd St., New York City, New York, under the Gretna Green Marriage Law (also the Quaker Law) prevailing at that time.

Kane then went on to the seas that always called to him. Although he carried her portrait with him, he often found himself in an unhappy state being away from Maggie, the only woman he ever loved; but, his explorations must continue. He wrote her letters and poetry and continuously reminded her to "avoid the spirits."

Kane, whose health was compromised, traveled to London to give a full report to Sir John Franklin's wife. From there he wrote Maggie that his health was not good and he would go to Havana to attempt to regain his health before meeting her in New York. The date and time had been set for Maggie and her mother to depart from New York to join him in Havana. But, as things seemed to go in Maggie's life, before their departure on Monday morning February 16, 1857, the news came of Kane's death at age 37. The bittersweet love story of Dr. Elisha Kane and Maggie Fox had ended in tragedy. Maggie was now a young widow.

Following Kane's death, Maggie found that for a time it was impossible to practice Spiritualism. A distraught Maggie turned to Catholicism, the faith of Dr. Kane. She attended St. Anne's Catholic Church. In August 1858, she became a member of St. Peter's Catholic Church. She felt this would keep her close to Kane. Although Maggie had her dear sister Katie close at hand most of the time, she felt she was left to face the world alone. She mourned for 14 years and then in a state of near poverty, she drifted back into the world she once knew—the world he said would be her lot—"a vocation of dreary and dissipated life." However, it was not all sad; there were some happy times along the way.

Note: The Love-Life of Dr. Kane: Containing the Correspondence, and a History of the Acquaintance, Engagement, and Secret Marriage Between Margaretta Fox and Elisha K. Kane. Authors listed as Dr. Elisha Kent Kane & Margaretta Fox published by Carlton Publishing, 1866.

IV

THE SPIRITUAL MANSION

Henry Seybert Finds A Medium

In Philadelphia, Pennsylvania, Mr. Henry Seybert once had a distinguished career in mineralogy but when his father passed, he never resumed his scientific studies again. His father left him a sizeable inheritance of investments and properties and it included a beautiful, fashionable mansion. Henry felt obligated to place most of his wealth into charitable and philanthropic purposes. His father's passing brought many questions to his saddened mind. Finally, he sought a medium for verification of his father's continued life. That medium was none other than Maggie Fox Kane. Henry became an enthusiastic adherent of the new movement of Spiritualism and its communication with the so-called dead.

The Spiritual Mansion

Henry found comfort in Spirit communication. He named his Philadelphia home The Spiritual Mansion (often shown as The Spiritualist Mansion once Maggie came on board). In 1871, Maggie, now thirty-four years old, entered into another chapter of her strange career. Finally removing the mourning garments she had worn for 14 long years in memory of the untimely termination of her dream of happiness, Maggie took up her new residency in the Spiritualist Mansion. She became known as "the Medium-in-Residency."

Maggie was now placed in the position of a professional life as a "medium," her only refuge that was left from a cruel existence of poverty and want. She was now on salary and appointments were more than plentiful. Many a young and ambitious medium would have loved to be in Maggie's position. Maggie became the high priestess of this new temple of unseen entities. She was honored and treated with the most exalted respect. At first, all of this attention was flattering and she enjoyed every moment of it. However, time has a way of changing all things. After some months as Medium of the Spiritual Mansion, the fame and glory seemed to dissipate.

Maggie was an excellent medium. She produced messages from the departed friends of her patrons and also from every martyr and saint in the Protestant calendar—from famous sages to rulers of old. But when it became a necessary requirement to transmit messages "demanded by the living of the apostles and fathers of the church," she revolted against this mania. She steadfastly refused to continue in her employment and complained that Henry Seybert was in the grip of "pure religious insanity."

Maggie left the Spiritual Mansion and all of the fame and glory in Philadelphia and returned to an apartment in New York City. She went back into her life of near nothingness and again succumbed to the influence of alcohol.

As time passed, things only got worse. Maggie was lost in the world of a reality created by her own confused mind.

In regard to Mr. Henry Seybert, perhaps there was a method to his madness. Maggie's guarded and in some measure candid course, no doubt tended very far towards influencing him to desire an honest and thorough investigation of the so-called Spiritualistic phenomena—one to be conducted according to the most rigid scientific methods. In his Last Will & Testament, he left a provision for the founding of a Chair of Philosophy in the University of Pennsylvania. He carefully stipulated that a certain portion of the income to be derived from the Foundation be devoted to the investigation of *"all systems of moral, religion or philosophy which assume to represent the truth;* **particularly Modern Spiritualism.**"

This legacy gave birth to the Seybert Commission (1883-1887). The commission was very biased and after many years of the study of outstanding mediums such as Maggie Fox Kane, Maud Laud, Henry Slade, P.L.O.A. Keeler, and James Mansfield, as well as many others, the committee released a report (1883) stating that "legerdemain (sleight of hand) and other artifices proved that psychic phenomena were the work of frauds." Being approached to further study, they released a final report in 1887 as well as a modification to that report eventually issued in 1920. Sadly, the only addition to both of these reports was a small preface of less than a full page. Certainly, this would have been distressing to Henry Seybert.

Today as we carefully review the Committee's actions, it is obvious that the Seybert Commission "never" met the requirements of the Last Will & Testament of Henry Seybert. The Last Will & Testament outlined specifically that which he desired be studied. When it came to Spiritualism, a reading of the reports clearly show that the committee studied only Spiritualism's phenomena, and it totally ignored its *"system of morals, religion or philosophy"*— that which was clearly stated in the Seybert Bequest.

V

God Has Not Ordered It

Confessions

The very first happening to start the ball rolling in the confession of Maggie and Katie began early in 1888. Reuben Briggs Davenport tells us that while Maggie was in London, the following appeared in one of the major newspapers in New York City:

THE NEW YORK HERALD
OF MAY 27, 1888

The Curse of Spiritualism, Gower Street, Bedford Square, W.C., London, Monday, May 14, 1888. To the Editor of the Herald:

I read in the Herald of Saturday, May 5, an account of the sad misfortune that has befallen my dear sister Katie, Mrs. Kate Fox Jencken, and in the article it is stated that I am still a resident of New York, which is a mistake. I sailed for England on the 22nd of March, and I presume my absence has added to my darling sister's depressed state of mind. The sad news had nearly killed me. My sister's two beautiful boys referred to are her idols.

SPIRITUALISM IS A CURSE. God has set His seal against it! I call it a curse, for it has made use of us as a covering for heartless persons like the Mme. Diss De Barrs, and the vilest miscreants make use of it to cloak their evil doings. Fanatics like Mr. Luther R. Marsh, Mr. John L. O'Sullivan, ex-Minister to Portugal, and hundreds equally as learned, ignore the 'rappings' (which is the only part of the phenomena that is worthy of notice) and rush madly after the glaring humbugs that flood New York. But a harmless 'message' that is given through the 'rappings' is of little account to them; they want the 'spirit' to come to them in full form, to walk before them, talk to them, to embrace them, and all such nonsense, and what is the result? Like old Judge Edmonds and Mr. Seybert of Philadelphia, they become crazed, and at the direction of their fraudulent 'mediums' they are induced to part with all their worldly possessions as well as their common sense, which God intended they should hold sacred. Mr. Marsh's experience is but another example of hundreds who have preceded him.

No matter in what form Spiritualism may be presented, it is, has been, and always will be a curse and a snare to all who meddle with it. No right minded man or woman can think otherwise.

I have found that fanatics are as plentiful among 'inferior men and women' as they are among the more learned. They are all alike. They cannot hold their fanaticism in check, and it increases as their years increase. All they will ever achieve for their foolish fanaticism will be loss of money, softening of the brains, and a lingering death."

/s/MARGARET (sic) F. KANE

Words such as these brought a deep shock to the hearts of many who had become sincere believers in the new movement that was said to have been founded by the Fox sisters. However, it did not stop there. Margaretta Fox Kane was interviewed upon her return from England in 1888. She told how she thought of suicide when traveling across the ocean aboard the ship named "Italy." She stated that the doctor, ship's Captain and some sailors prevented it. Once she had landed, she thanked them with heartfelt gratitude for saving her life. She gave of her "widow's mite'" to those wonderful men who saved her life.

Some 40 years later (1888) since the Hydesville rapping, both Katie and Maggie found themselves poorly provided for and lacking of worldly goods. Although Leah's husband Daniel had supported them financially and emotionally, Leah gave to them from her heart. However, Daniel and Leah were now distressed by both Maggie and Katie's continued use and abuse of alcohol. They were also upset that the sisters found no effort to be employed. Thus, Leah and Daniel stopped supporting them financially or emotionally. Alcohol appeared to be the sisters' only escape from reality and so it became prevalent in their lives. They were becoming more despondent about their so-called fraudulent profession. When Maggie returned from Europe in September 1888, she experienced terrible personal hardship. The media once again revealed her words with the following interview.

THE NEW YORK HERALD

Monday, September 24, 1888

"God has not Ordered It - One of the Fox Sisters Promises an Interesting Exposure of Fraud."

This headline startled both Spiritualists and non-Spiritualist alike. The story went on to tell how the celebrated medium, Capt. Elisha Kane's widow, stated that "Spirits never return."

Interviewer:

Since you now despise Spiritualism, how was it that you were engaged in it so long?

Maggie:

"Another sister of mine, and she coupled the name with an injurious adjective, made me take up with it. She's my damnable enemy. I hate her. My God! I'd poison her! No, I wouldn't but I'll lash her with my tongue. She was twenty-three years old the day I was born. I was an aunt seven years before I was born. Ha! Ha!

Yes, I am going to expose Spiritualism from its foundation. I have had the idea in my head for many a year, but I have never come to a determination before. I've thought of it day and night. I loath the thing I have been. As I used to say to those who wanted me to give a séance, 'You are driving me into hell.' Then the next day, I would drown my remorse in wine. I was too honest to remain a 'medium.' That's why I gave up my exhibitions.

When Spiritualism first began, Kate and I were little children, and this old woman (34) years, my older

God Has Not Ordered It

sister, made us her tools. Mother was a silly woman. She was a fanatic. I call her that because she was honest. She believed in these things.

Spiritualism started from just nothing. We were but innocent little children. What did we know? Ah, we grew to know too much!

Our sister used us in her exhibitions and we made money for her. Now she turns upon us because she's the wife of a rich man, and she opposes us both whenever she can. Oh, I am after her! You can kill sometimes without using weapons, you know.

Dr. Kane found me when I was leading this life [her voice trembled just here and she nearly broke down]. I was only thirteen (sic) when he took me out of it and placed me in school. I was educated in Philadelphia. When I was 16 (sic) years old he returned from the Arctic and we were married. Now comes the sad, sad tale. He was very ill. The physicians ordered him to London, but before he arrived he had a paralytic stroke of the heart. Then, he was sent back from London to Havana. Newsboys shouted in the streets of New York the news of his critical condition. Oh, my God! It was anguish to my ears! Mother and I were to have joined him in two weeks. He died before we arrived. Then I had brain fever. No one but God can know what sorrows I've had!

When I recovered, I was driven again into Spiritualism, and I gave exhibitions with my sister, Katie. I knew, of course, then, that every effect produced by us was absolute fraud. Why, I have explored the unknown as far as human will can. I have gone to the dead so that I might get from them some little token. Nothing ever came of it—nothing, nothing. I have been in graveyards of the dead at night, having permission to enter from those in charge. I have sat alone on a gravestone that the spirits of those who slept underneath might come to me. I have tried to obtain some sign. Not a thing! No, no, the dead shall not return, nor shall any that go down into hell. So says the Catholic Bible and so say I. The Spirits will not come back. God has not ordered it.

You want to know what the points of my exposé are. First, the 'rapping's' (sic)."

Note: Mrs. Kane paused here and I heard first a rapping under the floor near my feet, then under the chair in which I was seated, and again the same sound on the other side of it. Then, when she sat on the piano stool, the legs of the instrument reverberated more loudly, and the tap, tap, resounded throughout its hollow structure.

"It is all a trick? Absolutely. Spirits, is he not easily fooled? Rap, rap, rap! I can always get an affirmative answer to that question."

Interviewer:

Then I addressed certain suppositions to Maggie. A few seconds passed and then at last,

Maggie said:

"Yes, you have hit it. It is, as you say, the manner in which the joints of the foot can be used without lifting it from the floor. The power of doing this can only be acquired by practice begun in early youth.

One must begin as early as twelve years. Thirteen is rather late. We children, when we were playing together, years ago, discovered it, and it is my eldest sister who first put the discovery to such an infamous use. I call it infamous, for it was."

And, so the story began to unfold. Certainly, Maggie knew in her heart she was telling a horrible lie. However, despondent and under the effect of alcohol, the story rambled on. She, at that moment, believed **God had not ordained it.**

Reuben Briggs Davenport then reported that Maggie fulfilled her intention of publicly denouncing, with her own lips, Spiritualism and its attendant trickery.

VI

The Discomforted Enemy

The Next Story

The story continued to reach the general public through the newspapers. However, it was utterly surprising that not one Spiritualist attempted to refute the sad tale told by Maggie. Reuben Briggs Davenport then expressed Maggie's confession as "Mene, men, tekel, upharsin of Spiritualism." The translation is 'the handwriting on the wall.'

Certainly a response was expected from their sister, Leah Fox Underhill. After all, she had been the organizer, scheduler and promoter of the sisters and their newfound religion. Since she also had help in writing a book entitled <u>The Missing Link in Modern Spiritualism</u>, it was thought that for certain she would surely further justify Modern Spiritualism and all of its phenomena. But she remained silent! In fact, at the suggestion of Daniel Underhill, she packed her bags and went off to the country where she remained for several weeks. She felt secure at her brother David's place in Hydesville. There, she was safe from the inquisition of the reporters.

Daniel Underhill

It was a completely different reaction for her husband Daniel Underhill. Without communicating further with Leah about the issue, he agreed to discuss the subject with the media. Although he was publicly reluctant to being brought into the controversy, he spoke in a most uncomplimentary manner of Maggie but he did not evince any great amount of indignation when he said:

> *"I have for years helped both Maggie and Katie, and my wife has done everything in the world for them. We have furnished apartments for Maggie twice. They might both do well if they would only keep sober. Maggie can be as nice as you please or as vicious as a devil. Several persons have undertaken to manage her, but all have failed. Nobody can do anything with her. The first I knew that she was back in the city was through <u>The Herald.</u>*
>
> *I don't think she's in her right mind. I have done so much for her and she has behaved so badly in return that I have given her up now and will have nothing to do with her. She always says she will lecture, does she? Well, I don't believe she ever will. She's incapable of it.*
>
> *It is a great pity, though, that she should say such things about Spiritualism because of the odium which will result from it. But it isn't the first time she has said that she would declare against Spiritualism. She has had such spells before. It is astonishing to me that people have stuck to her and Katie as they have. It is all bosh about revealing the manner of producing the*

raps. I don't believe she can do it. I don't believe she knows how they are produced, except that it is done by an occult agency. Of course, there are frauds in Spiritualism. Mme. Diss De Barr was one of them. I don't believe much in materialization, but I've seen some real manifestations. They were in my own house. Nearly all my spiritualistic experience has been in my own house, and these sisters were the mediums.

Of course, Maggie's statement will be something of a shock to Spiritualists the world over, because they regard her and her sisters as the founders of their belief. In my opinion she is not accountable for what she says."

Although she had occasionally mentioned making that stand, the Underhills never believed Maggie would do what she had done. After getting Underhill's remarks, the reporters then turned to others seeking the position taken. They asked Mrs. E. A. Wells, another medium, who had provided fraudulent exhibitions for her input; the interview went as follows:

Interviewer:

"How have you regarded Mrs. Kane heretofore, Mrs. Wells."

Mrs. Wells:

"Why, with a good deal of respect as one of the first to get messages from the unseen world. The Fox sisters have a great name. I have no idea, though, if she really intends to do what she says she will do, that she's in her right senses."

The interviewer then went to another medium that had a wealthy clientele. At first she declined, not wanting to speak about another. But, she didn't hesitate to open the conversation.

Interviewer:

Did you hold the Fox sisters in much esteem as the pioneers of Spiritualism?

Medium:

"Yes I did, but personally knew nothing of them."

Interviewer:

Do you know Maggie has threatened exposure?

Medium (in great surprise)

"I don't believe she can expose any fraud. But if fraud exists, why, then, I say let it be exposed; the sooner the better. There's no fraud about me, that's very certain and I've some of the very best people in New York who come here.

I'll tell you what! I have heard that the Fox sisters are dreadfully addicted to drink. I don't know how far it is true, but I wouldn't believe anything she might say in any exposure. Maybe she's out of money and thinks the Spiritualists ought to do something for her... ."

Over time, interviews were obtained from wherever reporters could get someone to speak to them. Finally, a Spiritualist spoke! Mr. Henry J. Newton of the First Spiritual Society of New York offered the following:

"I had supposed all along that Mrs. Kane was still in Europe, and that she would never return to this country. I even heard at the time when Katie, her sister, was sent abroad, that Maggie was in Rome in the company of a well-known gentleman. I am very much surprised to know that she is in this city and more surprised that she threatens to make such silly pretended revelations as you say she proposes. They can only be revelations in name. She cannot reveal anything that can injure the Spiritualist's Cause or that will weaken in anyone's mind the truth of what we teach.

I have been absent in the country and have not read all that <u>The Herald</u> has published on this matter. I have read enough, however, to show me how utterly absurd and ridiculous her position is.

The idea of claiming that unseen 'rappings' can be produced with joints of the feet!! If she says this, even with regard to her own manifestations, she lies! I and many other men of truth and position have witnessed the manifestations of herself and her sisters many times under circumstances in which it was absolutely impossible for them to have been the least fraud.

Nothing that she could say in that regard would in the least change my opinion, nor would it that of anyone else who has become profoundly convinced that there is an occult influence connecting us with an invisible world.

I have seen Margaretta Fox Kane herself, when lying on a bed of sickness and unable to rise, produce 'rappings' in various parts of the room in which she was, and upon the ceilings, doors and windows several feet away from her. I have seen her produce the same effects when too drunk to realize what she was doing."

The interviews and rumors continued to flow. However, all those who had known Maggie had declared almost unanimously that she would not do such a thing if she had been in her right senses. They accused Maggie of excessive indulgence in alcohol and having become irresponsible. But then, although intended a death-blow to Spiritualism, Reuben Briggs Davenport concluded with the statement that "it is also recorded that while in London, she was known to have given some wonderful séances."

VII

The Second Blow

It appeared that even though the Spiritualists and non-Spiritualists alike had been in a state of shock, it all was finally beginning to subside. But then Mrs. Catherine Fox Jencken (Katie) arrived from Europe on October 9, 1888. She was not aware of what had taken place with her dear sister Maggie. Once it was made known to her, she immediately made it clear that her intention would be to support Maggie completely in her exposure of Spiritualism. This news was almost more than the Spiritualist's could handle. All they could hope for now was that Leah would not remain quiet. However, during her silence, the headlines on Wednesday, October 10, 1888, appeared:

AND KATY FOX NOW

The Youngest of the Mediumistic
Pioneers will Give the Snap Away

She arrives from Europe

Spiritualisms a Humbug from Beginning to End

Alleged Immoralities

"Katie Fox Jencken arrived yesterday from England on the Persian Monarch and she intends to cooperate fully with her sister—Margaretta Fox Kane—in her proposed exposé of the fraudulent method of so-called Spiritualism. Mrs. Jencken's coming was unexpected to Maggie, and it will certainly surprise the enemies of both.

The blow to Spiritualism which Maggie Fox struck not long ago caused a good deal more of consternation than Spiritualists generally have cared to confess. There is ample reason for stating that underneath a plausible surface of enforced calm there have been the hurried exchanges of forebodings and doubtings, and many consultations and goings to and fro. It is known that an overture was made to Maggie Fox suggestive of a money consideration for her silence, and that she rejected it with much indignation.

Mrs. Jencken walked into the parlor where Mrs. Kane was sitting about five o'clock yesterday and the sisters at once fell on each other's necks, in an ecstasy of affection and delight at being together once again. Mrs. Kane had just been talking to me about her projected lecture on 'The Curse of Spiritualism,' and Mrs. Jencken, who had heard nothing of the proposed exposé, except as it was casually rumored in her ear at the steamship dock, promptly gave her acquiescence to it as soon as she understood the situation. 'I do not care a fig for Spiritualism,' she said 'except so far as the good will of its adherents may affect the future of my boys. They are all I have in this life, and I live or die for them.' "

Additional trauma awaited Katie's arrival from England with her two sons, Ferdinand going on 16 and Henry, just 13 years old. With this new drama on the horizon of denouncing Spiritualism and the problems previously with the Children's Protective Agency, she feared they would once again attempt to take her children. She immediately sent them back to Europe. Katie was now free to continue her support of Maggie in denouncing Spiritualism.

However, her everloving public wrote many letters questioning the validity of the newspapers. One said: "Mrs. Jencken looks a far different person than she was when in deep trouble in this city and when she had to do with the rather unsympathetic measures of the Society for the Prevention of Cruelty to Children. No matron could bear a more placid and comely expression, and she declares with heartfelt earnestness that she is done forever with her once-besetting vice."

Interviewer:

Mrs. Jencken, are you willing to join with your sister in exposing the true modus operandi of Spiritualism?

Katie:

"I care nothing for Spiritualism. So far as I am concerned, I am done with it. I will say this; I regard it as one of the very greatest curses that the world has ever known. If I knew those powerful Spiritualists who have done their utmost to harm me in the past could not do so in the future, I would not hesitate a moment to expose it. The worst of them all is my eldest sister, Leah, the wife of Daniel Underhill. I think she was the one who caused my arrest last spring and the bringing of the preposterous charge against me that I was cruel to my children and neglectful of them. I don't know why it is, she has always been jealous of Maggie and me; I suppose because we could do things in Spiritualism that she couldn't."

Interviewer:

Why don't you come squarely out, then, with the truth, and make the public your friends? You needn't fear any persecution if you do that.

Katie:

"Well, if my sister's (Maggie) health was only fully restored and I knew she was fully herself, I would certainly join her in showing Spiritualism to be what it really is. I want to be sure of that, however, I want the thing done properly when it is done."

Interviewer:

Then you will not deny that what she has said of Spiritualism is true?

Katie:

"I will not deny it. Spiritualism is a humbug from beginning to end. It is the greatest humbug of the century. I don't know whether she had told you this, but Maggie and I started it as very little children, too young, too innocent, to know what we were doing. Our sister Leah was twenty-three years older than either of us. We got started in the way of deception, and being encouraged in it, we went on, of course. Others, old enough to have been ashamed of the infamy, took us out into the world. My sister Leah has published a book called <u>The Missing Link in</u>

Modern Spiritualism. It professes to give the true history of this movement, so far as it originated with us. Now, there's nothing but falsehood in that book from beginning to end, excepting the fact that Horace Greeley educated me. The rest is nothing but a string of lies."

Interviewer:

And about the manifestation at Hydesville in 1848 and the finding of bones in the cellar and so on?

Katie:

"All humbuggery, every bit of it. And yet, Maggie and I are the founders of Spiritualism!"

Many stories exist of the séances and the wonderful phenomena demonstrated in the London home of the Scottish satirical writer of the Victorian era, Thomas Carlyle. The next day the interviewer once again began by asking –

Interviewer:

The English papers have been filled with stories, more or less skeptical, regarding the queer occurrences in Carlyle's home in Chelsea, London.

Katie:

"All that took place there of that nature is utterly false. I haven't the slightest idea that the noises which we heard in the house had any connection with Carlyle's spirit. I certainly know that every so-called manifestation produced through me in London or anywhere else was a fraud. Many a time have I wept because when I was young and innocent I was brought into such a life. The time has now come for Maggie and I to set ourselves right before the world. Nobody knows at what moment either of us might be taken away. We ought not to leave this base fabric of deceit behind us unexposed."

Maggie was well prepared for the exposé but now that the time was near at hand, her nerves became frazzled. It is said that on Sunday, October 21, 1888, Maggie appeared at the Academy of Music in New York City before a distinguished audience and without reserve demonstrated the falsity of all that she had done in the guise of mediumship. She stood before the footlights trembling with intense feeling and made the solemn abjuration of Spiritualism while Katie Fox Jencken sat in a neighboring box giving her consent to Maggie's every word.

Maggie began:

"That I have been chiefly instrumental in perpetrating the fraud of Spiritualism upon a too confiding public, most of you doubtless know. The greatest sorrow of my life has been that this is true, and though it has come later in my day, I am now prepared to tell the truth, the whole truth and nothing but the truth—so help me God. There are probably many here who will scorn me for the deception I have practiced, yet did they know the true history of my unhappy past, the living agony and shame that it has been to me, they would pity, not reproach. The imposition which I have so long maintained began in my early childhood, when with character and mind still unformed, I was unable to distinguish right and wrong. I repented it in my

maturity. I have lived through years of silence through intimidation, scorn, and bitter adversity concealing as best I might the consciousness of my guilt. Now, thanks to God and my awakened conscience I am at last able to reveal the fatal truth, the exact truth of this hideous fraud which has withered many hearts and has blighted so many hopes in lives. I am here tonight as one of the founders of Spiritualism, to denounce it as an absolute falsehood from beginning to end, as the flimsiest superstition, the most wicked blasphemy known to the world. I ask only your kind attention and forgiveness, and as I may prove myself worthy by the step I am now taking, may you extend to me your helping hands and sustain me in the better path I have chosen."

A large number of Spiritualists had created a disturbance during the talk in an attempt to create a diversion that would break the tone of the cruel words by Maggie Fox. However, they failed in their attempt. Both Maggie and Katie turned the world of Spiritualism into a frenzy. The Spiritualists knew, without a doubt, the girls were true mediums and the raps were from the Spirit side of life. They could only wonder what brought about this terrible happening. However, at the moment, Maggie was well satisfied within herself. In her mind, she had set the record straight. She was more than pleased with the opportunity to grace the stage of the prestigious Academy of Music in New York City. Her heart swelled in knowing that her dear sister Katie stood behind her 100 percent in her total denunciation of that which they had founded 40 years ago. It was now felt they had done their job and performed well. Surely, all of the newspaper reports and their testimonies would be the final **Death-blow to Spiritualism**.

VIII
"The Recantation"

Years 1888 & 1889

It is true that which has been said time and time again, that 'time' changes all things. This was true with <u>The Death-Blow to Spiritualism</u> written by Reuben Briggs Davenport in 1888. Now just one year later in November **1889**, Davenport's death-blow became discredited because Maggie recanted the whole gory story to which she and Katie once had signed to be true. Should Davenport take all the blame? Probably so, for he knew both women were deeply and continuously under the influence of alcohol. He only used that timing to fortify his views against Spiritualism.

Recantation

Although the news of the recantation spread rapidly in 1889, it continued to make the news over and over again. Spiritualists wanted the world to know that the curse by Maggie and Katie was fiction, not fact. One such printing was issued again four years later on Saturday, March 25, 1893, in <u>The Banner of Light</u>. It carried a repeat of the recantation of Mrs. Margaretta Fox Kane. It is printed here for all to see; Maggie's words are in italics.

THE BANNER OF LIGHT

Boston, Saturday, March 25, 1893

MRS. KANE'S RECANTATION

Copy of Statement made by
Mrs. Margaret (sic) FoxKane, November, 1889.

"A few days before the following statement was made by Mrs. Kane, I met her on 6th Avenue—it seemed by chance, although she remarked, 'Oh! Mrs. Newton, I do believe the good angels have sent me to you.' I had not seen her for many months; not for some time. She seemed very repentant for the course she had pursued; gave me her address, and wished Mr. Newton and myself to call upon her, and she would tell us all about it. On my return home, I related to Mr. Newton an account of my interview with Mrs. Kane. He said it was our religious duty, as Spiritualists, to stand by Mrs. Kane, especially if she was repentant, for we, in common with hundreds, yes, thousands, could testify to the genuineness of the 'raps' as given through her mediumship; for it is the unmistakable individual intelligence that is conveyed, and not wholly the raps themselves that carries conviction.

Mr. Newton felt that it was of great importance to the Cause and especially to the history of Spiritualism, that a true statement should be made by Mrs. Kane of the influences that had persuaded her to take the course she did. Mr. Newton called upon her, taking with him Mr. C. P. Sykes. It was then arranged that she should come to our house, and, in the presence of a stenographer, make her statement.

The following is a true copy of that statement by Magaretta Fox Kane."

/s/Mary A. Newton

THE RECANTATION
by Maggie Fox Kane

"Would to the injustice I did the Cause of Spiritualism, when, under the strong psychological influence of persons who were opposed to it, I gave expression to utterances that had no foundation in fact, and that would at the time throw discredit on the spiritual phenomena. If an unreserved denial of all I then said derogatory of it can, in any way, make amends for the wrong I did, I most gladly do so. This is no mere idle use of words with me. For months past, I have suffered unspeakable anguish, and I now feel the most poignant regret for the ruinous course I was made to follow. It is not of my own volition that I have decided upon this course, because of myself I would wish to remain in the quiet of a secluded life, away from the criticism and abuse that are likely to be hurled at me from all sides.

As I said, this retraction and denial has not come about so much from my own sense of what is right, as from the silent impulse of the spirits using my organism. Of myself, I would wish to avoid the 'slings and arrows' from friends turned enemies perhaps on the one side, and the treacherous horde who held out promises of wealth and happiness in return for an attack on

Spiritualism, and whose hopeful assurances were so deceitful. But I will earnestly persevere in the course that has been marked out for me by my spirit guides, and I will make the most earnest endeavor to be true to my heavenly inspirers, and to serve the Cause I unconsciously abused in such a vehement manner."

Interviewer:

When (Mrs. Kane was asked) did you decide to explain the position which you were made to take to the alleged exposé?

Maggie said:

"It is not of recent date," she replied. "It is months since I was first urged to do this thing. I did my utmost to repress the uncontrollable desire to make a clean breast of the whole treacherous onslaught on Spiritualism, but try as I might, the irrepressible spiritual influence urged me to this course with greater vigor."

Interviewer:

Do you not think that this silent influence might be more accurately described as a 'spirit of revenge' for blasted hopes of a rich reward for your own treachery?

Maggie:

"It cannot be. If I could consult my own desires I would not again come before the public. So far as a 'feeling of revenge' being a factor in the premises, that idea can be very easily set at rest by the fact that there is no way by which I could bring the miscreants and plotters of evil

to retribution; besides, of myself, I am resigned to my sad lot and harbor no ill will."

Interviewer:

But you say you will go upon the platform and by that means make matters even with your quondam* friends.

Maggie:

"I shall enter upon a tour of lecturing, but my intentions are far from what you suppose them to be. My only purpose is to declare to the world that I was under a baneful influence when I made my attack on Spiritualism, and to right a wrong."

Interviewer:

You say that you, being the best-known exponent of the phenomena of Spiritualism, were psychologized by the enemies of that religion with the object of doing it an injury. How do you know that some Spiritualist may not be adopting the same method to secure this retraction of your former attitude?

Maggie:

"I am perfectly aware of the fact that it is not the case. Long before I spoke to any person on this matter, I was unceasingly reminded by my spirit-controls what I had to do, and at last I have come to the conclusion that it would be useless for me to further thwart their promptings."

---

*Note: Definition of Quondam – "belonging to some prior time; "erstwhile friend"; "our former glory."

Interviewer:

Were there no overtures made by a spirit in the flesh?

Maggie:

"No. I will tell you how I came to make it known to my people, as I like to speak of the Spiritualists. I was walking on Sixth (sic) Avenue, in this city one day, when I met Mrs. Henry J. Newton. The meeting was altogether apparently accidental, but I do believe it was brought about by the intervention of the 'good spirits,' and I told Mrs. Newton so; this was, I am sure the work of the angel-world; and though I disliked very much to intrude my theme of sorrow on any person, I could not disobey the will of the spirits. I related to her some of the facts concerning the whole affair. It struck me forcibly the look on Mrs. Newton's face when she heard me speak about the 'good spirits.' Subsequently, an arrangement was made to meet at Mr. Newton's house and the result is that I meet you tonight."

Interviewer:

Has there been no mention of a monetary consideration for this statement?

Maggie:

"Not the smallest; none whatever."

Interviewer:

Then financial gain is not the end which you are looking for?

Maggie:

"Indirectly, yes. My great ambition is to repair the wrong I have done; but you know that even a mortal instrument in the hands of the spirits must have the maintenance of life. This I propose to derive from my lectures. Not one cent has passed to me from any person because I adopted this course."

Interviewer:

What cause led up to your exposure of the spirit-rapping?

Maggie:

"At the time, I was in great need of money and persons who for the present I prefer not to name, took advantage of the situation; hence, the trouble. The excitement, too, helped to upset my equilibrium."

Interviewer:

What was the object of the persons who induced you to make the statement that you and all mediums traded in the credulity of the people?

Maggie:

"They had several objects in view; their first and paramount idea was to crush Spiritualism to make money for themselves, and to get up a great excitement, as that was an element in which they flourished."

Interviewer:

Since you passed out from public view, what have you been engaged in?

Maggie:

"In misery. The tide of my affairs was changed when I fell a victim to false friends, and I made that denunciation. I have known nothing but calamity, want and suffering since. Unceasing remorse has made it evident to me that it is time I should take a decided stand in the matter, and let the truth be known."

Interviewer:

Was there any truth in the charges you made against Spiritualism?

Maggie:

"Those charges were false in every particular. I have no hesitation in saying that."

Interviewer:

Am I to understand from you that the spirits have not deserted you?

Maggie:

"On the contrary, their manifestations are more powerful than ever. At times they are so demonstrative as to cause annoyance to an old lady on the same floor with me."

Interviewer:

Won't you name any of those who were instrumental in causing you to make such sweeping charges against the methods of your people?

Maggie:

"I do not wish to just now; but I will mention that persons high in the Catholic Church did their best to have me enter a convent."

Interviewer:

Was the offer made by any one in this country?

Maggie:

"No. In London. I had a letter from Cardinal Manning advising me to abandon this 'wicked work of the devil.'"

Interviewer:

A year ago, when you were dealing your 'death-blow' to Spiritualism, you said it would prove a curse to any one having anything to do with it. Your opinion is changed, of course.

Maggie:

"No. My belief in Spiritualism has undergone no change. When I made those dreadful statements, I was not responsible for my words. Now that I have got rid of the terrible incubus which enthralled my every word and action, my belief in the philosophy and the phenomena, too, mind you, of Spiritualism is unshaken. Its genuineness is an incontrovertible fact. Not all the Hermanns (sic) that ever breathed the breath of life can duplicate the wonders that are produced through some mediums. By adeptness of fingers and smartness of wits they may produce writing on paper and slates, but even this cannot bear close inspection. Materialization is beyond the mental caliber to reproduce, and I

challenge any one to make the 'raps' under the same condition as I will. There is not a human being on earth can produce the 'raps' in the same was (sic) as they are made through me."

Interviewer*:*

Do you propose to hold séances?

Maggie*:*

"No. I will devote myself entirely to platform work, as that will give me a better opportunity to refute the foul slanders uttered by me against Spiritualism."

Interviewer*:*

Won't you be good enough to say who was chief conspirator?

Maggie:

"Well, as you are so persistent, I will name the Roman Catholic Church, through some of its representatives."

Interviewer*:*

But, surely, the increase of Spiritualism would not mean harm to that church any more than to other churches.

Maggie:

"You know it hates everything opposed to its tenets, and will not spare any means to blot from existence any person or sect that does not agree with its doctrines. Selfishness and hatred, I suppose, were the motives by which those Catholics were actuated. But this effort was made by a powerful society of that persuasion in London."

Interviewer:

What does your sister Katie say of your present course?

Maggie:

"She is in complete sympathy with me. She did not approve my course in the past."

Interviewer

Since you have unburdened your mind of the trouble which weighed upon it, how do you feel? Have you no compunction for your latest move?

Maggie:

"I feel no remorse but for that which I did when I was unconsciously made the tool of moral pirates and traducers of a holy cause. Now that I have taken this step, my heart feels lighter, and I am glad. I no longer suffer the hellish torments which constantly racked my mental and physical being."

Interviewer:

Did not your sister sign a paper endorsing your abuse of Spiritualism?

Maggie:

"It is possible she may have done so; but such signature must have been secured by fraudulent devices and misrepresentations. She has always been an unfaltering Spiritualist."

Interviewer:

Will you have a manager for your lecture tour?

Maggie:

"No, sir. I have a horror of them. They, too, treated me most outrageously. Frank Stechen acted shamefully with me. He made considerable money through his management for me, and left me in Boston without a cent. All I got from him was five hundred and fifty dollars, which was given to me at the beginning of the contract."

Interviewer:

You seem to have a dread of newspapers and notoriety and editors.

Maggie:

"I have. The editors of some of the great dailies did not treat me fairly. Of the reporters, I will say that I know when I was placed prominently, but unenviably, before the public, three-fourths of them were avowed believers in Spiritualism."

Interviewer:

You are sure that money is not your predominating purpose in taking back what you said?

Maggie:

"It is only a secondary consideration. I do not want it to be understood that I am regardless of the value of money. The want of it is a curse, and any one who says it is not so cannot be sincere. Money enables us to be true to ourselves, and is one of the greatest blessings. Where a medium is indigent and in want, the manifestations of the spirits will not amount to much; but if the

mental condition is all right, and she is not troubled about her earthly well-being, the best results will be obtained."

Interviewer:

Then you have resumed your old self since you came from under the bad psychological control?

Maggie:

"Most undoubtedly. In fact, I am more determined and firmer in my faith and I shall put forth every endeavor to proclaim the truth of Spiritualism, the belief in which has never weakened in me; past experience has made it as hard as adamant."

To give greater authenticity to the interview, at her suggestion the following open letter was written, to which Maggie placed her signature:

128 West 43d Street
New York City, Nov. 16th, 1889

TO THE PUBLIC: The foregoing interview having been read over to me, I find nothing contained therein that is not a correct record of my words and truthful expression of my sentiments. I have not given a detailed account of the ways and means which were devised to bring me under subjection, and so extract from me a declaration that the spiritual phenomena as exemplified through my organism were a fraud. But I shall fully atone for this incompleteness when I get upon the platform.

(Signed) MARGARET (sic) FOX-KANE

Witnesses: Henry J. Newton, Mary A. Newton, John L. O'Sullivan, (Former U.S. Minister to Portugal).

IX

Life Goes On

Final Shot At <u>The Death-Blow To Spiritualism</u>

Now that Maggie had recanted on her original curse of Spiritualism, life could go on. It was late in 1889 when she returned to the platform and once again gave the phenomenal demonstrations of the mediumship exhibited in her youth. Katie followed in the footsteps of her dearest sister. <u>The Death-Blow to Spiritualism</u> written by Reuben Briggs Davenport failed.

The Rifts Worsened

The rifts between the sisters and Leah and her husband Daniel had only widened as time passed. Although Leah had patiently continued in begging her sisters to leave the alcohol alone, it was all for naught. The time came that she felt there was no recourse but to just give up. In total despair, disgust, and a heavy heart, she finally closed the door forever. There could be no bridge long enough to span the hurt that separated the sisters' lives. Sadly, they were never to be in each other's lives again.

Maggie and Katie continued to make what little livelihood they could by holding private séances, readings, and speaking engagements in between their frightening bouts with alcohol. However, it was never enough to support them in a proper manner.

Leah and David's Final Meeting

It was August 1890 when Leah made what she considered her very last trip to the home place she loved in Hydesville. Through all the years of their lives, Leah and her brother David had always been so very close. She not only loved David and her sister-in-law Elizabeth dearly but their children were very special to her. In fact, Leah and Daniel had raised three of David and Elizabeth's children.

Now at last, even though her heart was heavy, at best she was home again. Leah and David spent long hours talking honestly with each other as they always had done. After several days had passed and after much deep thought, Leah had decided not to return to her home and husband in New York. David, acting as the big brother that he had always been, emphatically told her that she must go back. She didn't have a choice in the matter. He told her she must put her pride aside and go and make peace with their younger sisters, Maggie and Katie. Although she impatiently tried to interrupt him more than once, he kept her silenced. She listened intently as the tears came very close to rolling down her cheeks...this was just what he wanted. After a little more conversation, David said: "Leah, do as I say—go back and help them. They need your love now—more than they ever needed it before." He then looked directly into her eyes and asked her for a promise. Without a single word from her lips, she embraced him knowing deep in her heart it was their last goodbye.

Leah arrived home downhearted, tired, and worn. The next day, on Saturday, November 1, 1890, she noticed her beautiful porcelain vase was missing from its place on the ornate mantle. She immediately questioned the head housekeeper. Although somewhat hesitant, she admitted the new servant had broken it as it was far too heavy for her to lift. Leah's face first paled, then a burning fury filled her being. Her flooded rage cut off her breath and she fell to the floor—silenced, never to speak again. Leah is interred in the Underhill Family Plot in Green-Wood Cemetery in Brooklyn, New York, a cemetery for the rich and famous.

Catherine (Katie)

Time moved along, and her dear friends, the Taylors, returned from their three years abroad. Although, they longed to see Katie, finding her was a major disappointment. Her physical weakness was rapidly advancing. However sick as she was, her mediumship was as strong as ever and she gave messages that brought forth tears from Sarah Taylor's eyes. As always, the Taylors wanted to help Katie but as always she refused. They parted not knowing if they would meet again. This parting created a year of silence since Katie had moved and had not contacted them. Sarah prayed daily that she might find Katie again.

Caring for his very sick mother and knowing her weakness all too well, Ferdinand was overprotective of her. Some months had passed and although Ferdinand was with his mother most of the time, she somehow obtained liquor in spite of his constant watch. On Saturday, July 2, 1892, Ferdinand went off to work leaving his mother sleeping but a flash of intuition sent him back home only to find her dead. Catherine Fox Jencken had made her transition at 53 years of age at 609 Columbia Avenue in Brooklyn, N.Y. Ferdinand hunted for Maggie but she was nowhere to be found so he turned to Sarah. He did not have the means to take care of his mother's burial.

Titus Merritt, a dear friend of the family for many years, took care of Katie. He had Katie's physical remains placed in a holding vault in Green-Wood Cemetery, Brooklyn. He faithfully paid the statement each month to provide a place for her there.

Katie Fox Jencken was survived by her oldest son, Ferdinand L. D. Jencken. Following in his mother's footsteps, he, too, had his bouts with alcoholism and was not dependable. In fact, he received help in securing jobs as well as receiving financial assistance from the newly formed organization, The National Spiritualist Association. The fact that he was married with a second child due soon necessitated his working a regular job. Once again, members of the newly formed organization spoke in his behalf to help him secure employment.

Margaretta (Maggie)

As would be expected, Maggie became extremely despondent over the passing of her dear sister, Katie. Where else could she turn but to alcohol? Just eight months after

Katie's passing, Joseph La Fume sat by her bedside at the home of a close friend. He sat there in deep, sad retrospection. For many months, he had provided Maggie's wants and needs. Although she lay unconscious from time-to-time, Joseph came to be with her every day. He had always loved Maggie but feeling that it would not be accepted, he kept his feelings in check.

One Last Look

It was now Wednesday, March 8, 1893, and Maggie was slipping away. But she opened her eyes and Joseph looked into them not believing the vibrancy and beauty, free of the drug's usual reaction. There was a blissful smile on her old but sweet face. At 4:30 a.m. a heart attack let her slip away in a flash at age 56 at the home of her friend, Emily B. Ruggles at 492 State Street, Brooklyn, New York. Spirit raps continued for several minutes after her death. Ferdinand would take responsibility and notify the few remaining relatives. Maggie's body must have a proper burial and that would be the last gift Joseph La Fume could give to his long time friend and secret love. He met with Ferdinand and offered a place for Maggie in his family plot. On Saturday, March 11, 1893, Maggie was interred in Sec. 3, Lot 355 in Cypress Hills Cemetery, Brooklyn, New York.

Margaretta & Catherine Together Again

Joseph La Fume's last deed was yet to be done. Since Katie's passing on July 2, 1892, Titus Merritt had generously paid the monthly fee to the Green-Wood Cemetery to assure Katie's remains a safe haven in the holding vault. Joseph knew the love the sisters had for each other and felt they must be together in death just as they were there for each other in life. He took the responsibility as his very own and made the necessary arrangements with both cemeteries. On Tuesday, December 12, 1893, Joseph La Fume had Katie's remains removed from the holding vault in Green-Wood Cemetery, Brooklyn, N.Y. and had her interred in the same grave with her beloved sister, Maggie, in Cypress Hills Cemetery, Brooklyn.

Spiritualism's founders were now on the higher side of life. However, the story does not end there.

X

Light From Beyond The Tomb

The Death-Blow To Spiritualism by Reuben Briggs Davenport could not survive once the flicker of the "Recantation" by Maggaretta Fox Kane began to burn. Nor did it survive after the passing of either Maggie or Katie. Life teaches us to be patient—things are sure to change.

The good demonstration of mediumship by Maggie and Katie had prevailed from childhood far into their adulthood. They worked tediously to provide the seeker communication from their loved ones in world beyond. They brought comfort to many that were bereaved. They led many others to the understanding of a continuity of life. Because of their mediumship, many came to believe in communication with the so-called dead. Others joined the growing movement now known as Modern American Spiritualism. Then there were others who perhaps may have still pondered:

* Perhaps the paths that the Fox sisters took through their lifetime caused some to doubt the truth of the phenomena.
* Perhaps to others the validity of the happenings on March 31, 1848, was still questioned—but truth finally came.

* Perhaps the sisters did offer hope to many during times of darkness.
* Perhaps the voices from the grave shed light on the truth that they still lived.
* Perhaps it caused many others to become believers.
* Perhaps too, to some Spiritualism was a Truth and became their way of life and 'the way' for many others they touched.

The question of whether or not communication occurred with the Spirit of the peddler and the Fox Sisters had often been a topic of debate. Did it really happen? Could it be possible? Eleven long years elapsed after the passing of Maggie Fox Kane before the "final answer" came as a light from beyond the tomb.

The headlines of the newspaper of the day caught the attention of many from all walks of life. Spiritualists rejoiced! Reuben Briggs Davenport's <u>The Death-Blow of Spiritualism</u> *was finally killed!* The headlines of the <u>Boston Journal</u>, Thursday, November 23, 1904, caught the attention of many. It read as follows:

BONES IN "OLD SPOOKHOUSE"

Apparent Confirmation of the Story Told
by Originators of Spiritualism.

Newark, N.Y., Nov 22—"William H. Hyde, owner of what was known as the "Old Spook House," has discovered human bones under the cellar wall, which had fallen in as the result of being undermined by running water.

It was in the "Old Spook House" at Hydesville, Wayne County, N.Y., that the Fox Sisters, daughters of Mr. and Mrs. John D. Fox, started the movement which has resulted in Modern Spiritualism.

The Fox family occupied the house in the late eighteen (sic) forties. In 1848, the family was unbearably disturbed by certain mysterious "knocks" and "raps." It is alleged that at length Kate Fox, one of the two daughters, discovered that the cause of the sounds was intelligent, and that questions asked would be answered by the number of raps, "one for no and three for yes."

There is absolutely no doubt that the Fox girls declared that the rappings proceeded from the Spirit of a certain peddler, whose throat had been cut by a previous tenant of the house, and whose body had been buried in the cellar.

An investigation of the matter seemed to show that none of the Fox family produced the rappings. Efforts were made to find the body of the peddler, but they were unsuccessful, probably because of the quantity of running water that was encountered when digging in the cellar began.

It was at Rochester, where the two Fox girls afterward went to live with a married sister, Mrs. Fish, that Modern Spiritualism assumed its present form, and that communication was, it was asserted, established with the Spirits of inquirers' relatives and with the dead eminent man. Kate Fox and her sister were the first "mediums."

And another news article in the Rochester Democrat in 1904:

Rochester, N.Y. Nov. 22: "The skeleton of the man supposed to have caused the rapping first heard by the Fox Sisters in 1848 has been found in the walls of the house occupied by the sisters, and clears them from any shadow of doubt held concerning their sincerity in the discovery of Spirit communication.

The Fox sisters declared they learned to communicate with the Spirit of a man, and that he told them he had been murdered and buried in the cellar. Repeated excavations failed to locate the body, and thus give proof positive of their story.

The discovery was made by school-children playing in the cellar of the building in Hydesville known as the 'Spook House,' where the Fox sisters heard the wonderful rappings. William H. Hyde, a reputable citizen of Clyde, who owns the house, made an investigation and found an almost entire human skeleton between the earth and crumbling cellar walls, undoubtedly that of the wandering peddler who it claimed was murdered in the east room of the house and whose body was hidden in the cellar.

Mr. Hyde has notified relatives of the Fox sisters, and the notice of the discovery will be sent to the National Order of Spiritualists, many of whom remember having made pilgrimage to the 'Spook House,' as it is commonly called. The finding of the bones practically corroborates the sworn statement made by Margaret (sic) Fox, April 1848."

And yet another article printed in both the

ROCHESTER
DEMOCRAT & CHRONICLE,
Wed. Nov 23, 1904

Human Bones Discovered
Found Under Famous Fox House at Newark.

"Spirits Right"

The Find Corroborates an Old Story
Was a Man Murdered?

"It was claimed by the Fox family in 1848 that Spirits told them there were bones under the house.

Present discovery of significance to Spiritualists.

Newark, Nov. 22 — William H. Hyde, a well-known citizen of Newark and the owner of the old spook house in which modern (sic) spiritualism (sic) originated March 31, 1848, reported a startling discovery today. Mr. Hyde while at the house Sunday discovered human bones consisting of vertebrae, rib, arm and leg bones, a shoulder blade and collar bone. It seems that the north (sic) cellar wall of the old house fell in recently and as a result the bones were exposed. A little boy in the neighborhood reported to Mr. Hyde the other day that his grandfather had seen some bones at the house. Mr. Hyde went to the scene after dinner Sunday and in an interview with your correspondent said that water had washed out the foundation of the wall on the north (sic) side of the house. The wall fell in under the doorsill, under which there was found a two-foot space where the bones were discovered.

Considerable significance will be attached to this discovery by Spiritualists. According to the authenticated story of Spiritualism, John D. Fox and his family moved into the house December 11, 1847. In a few months the family began to be disturbed nights by unusual noises which sounded like someone rapping. It was impossible to locate the sounds, which resembled the furniture being moved, but on examination the furniture was always found to be in perfect order. There were two children living at home, Margaretta (sic) and Catherine (sic), twelve (sic) and nine respectively, and the noises so alarmed the parents that it was finally thought best to have the children sleep in the room with them.

The very night after this arrangement had been made, the household was again disturbed and the entire house searched. The noises continued and were heard in the same place. They were not loud but produced a jar of the bedstead and chairs. On March 30th, the family was disturbed all night, the noise being heard in various parts of the house. Mr. Fox stationed himself outside of the door while his wife stood inside and the knocks came on the door between them. Footsteps were heard in the pantry and downstairs and the couple concluded the house must be haunted.

A Memorable Night

On the memorable night of March 31, 1848, the family retired early, determining not to permit themselves to be disturbed by the noises and intending to get a good night's rest. The noises commenced again as usual after the family retired and the children heard rappings and tried to make similar noises by snapping their fingers. According to the statement of the mother, which is published in <u>The Missing Link</u> (sic), the oldest child, Maggie, said: 'Now, do as I do.' Clapping her hands, at which the sounds instantly followed her with the same number of claps.

When she stopped, the sound ceased for a time, then Margaretta (sic) said in sport: 'Now do as I do, count one, two, three, four,' striking one hand against the other at the same time, when the mysterious raps came as before. The child was afraid to repeat this, when Cathy (sic) said that she thought the next day was April Fool day, and that somebody was trying to fool them. The mother then thought of testing the noise in a way that no one in the house could answer and asked for her children's ages successively, when each was correctly given. Various questions were asked and answered, and the spirit finally divulged the fact that a man aged 31 had been murdered in the house and that his remains were buried in the cellar.

Neighbors who were called in, and saw the children pale with fright and nearly speechless, were amazed. Several neighbors remained in the house all night, and on the next Saturday the house was filled to overflowing. On Sunday noises were heard throughout the entire day, and April 1st they commenced digging in the cellar, but on striking water had to give up, although later, in a dry time, according to the story, human bones were found. The cottage is near Ganargua Creek or Mud Creek, and the successful digging took place 1 July when the water had subsided.

Scouted the Idea

Now while these facts have been accredited by Spiritualists, townspeople heretofore scouted the idea of anyone ever having been murdered in the cottage. But Mr. Hyde's discovery of Sunday is corroborative evidence that cannot be controverted. The bones were actually found outside of the cellar, and but for the falling of the wall might never have been unearthed.

All of the Fox family is now deceased, the last member, Maria Fox Smith, whose decease occurred in November 1902. The most noted member of the family was the oldest child, Leah, who had married three times, to a Mr. Fish, a Mr. Brown, and to her last husband Daniel Underhill whose name she carried at her death in 1890, when her remains were buried in Green-Wood cemetery. At the time of the famous Spiritualist rappings she was living in Rochester, her name being Fish at that time. She made her name famous by publishing the notable work, <u>The Missing Link in Modern Spiritualism</u> by A. Leah Underhill of the Fox family.

Tourists and sightseers from all parts of the country visit Newark frequently to view the house where Spiritualism originated, and its adherents hold it in veneration. A souvenir spoon with a picture of the house was sold at the World's Fair. The owner Mr. Hyde, intends to keep the house in a state of preservation as long as possible. It is believed that the house was built in 1815 but by whom is not known. The frame is about 20 x 24 feet, and it is located about two miles north of the village on the well known Hydesville Road. It has not been occupied for many years."

The prestigious **New York Times** of Nov. 24, 1904

HEADLESS SKELETON
IN FOX SISTERS HOME

House in Which the Spiritualists
Resided Had Double Foundation

MARGARET'S MURDER STORY

"Medium" Insisted That Slain Man's Spirit
Told Her His Body was Buried in Cellar

Special to the New York Times.

ROCHESTER, N.Y. Nov 23—"In the cellar of the little house located on the farm of W. H. Hyde, in the hamlet of Hydesville, one mile north of the village of Newark, where the Fox sisters resided in 1848, the year which witnessed the birth of Modern Spiritualism, human bones have been found. They are believed to be the bones of Charles Rosna (sic), who, according to the sworn statement made by Margaret (sic) Fox, was the man whose spirit made the rappings, and who communicated to her by a system of rappings the story of his murder in the house by a man named Bell and the burial of his body in the cellar of the house.

Time and again the cellar of this house had been dug up in search for the bones which were the missing link in the Fox Sisters story. Why they were not found before is now made clear.

On Sunday, children playing in the cellar found a few bones and took them to W. H. Hyde, son of Artemus Hyde, who rented the house to the Fox family in 1847. Hyde thought they were human bones, and made an investigation. He began digging, and found out something he did not know before—that the house had two separate stone foundations. The outer walls are complete in themselves that support the house, the frame extending over on all sides, and the surface being filled in with earth up to the framework. Two feet inside of this foundation are the second walls, the space having been filled in with earth. Recent rain had weakened the inner walls, and on Sunday, while the children were playing in the cellar, the wall gave way revealing the bones.

Mr. Hyde began digging and near the doorway on the north side found human bones, consisting of vertebrae, rib, arm, and leg bones, a shoulder blade and collar bone. They had been buried between the two walls, and as earlier excavations had been merely up to the inner wall, of course, were not discovered.

Today, Mr. Hyde did some more digging, and after a thorough search found enough bones to make an almost complete skeleton, the head, however, being missing. Margaret (sic) Fox affirmed that the spirit of the murdered man told her that the head had been severed from the body, placed in a stovepipe and thrown into the creek near the house.

Mr. Hyde now has the bones at his residence and has notified relatives of the Fox family living in the vicinity. Notice has also been sent to the National Order of Spiritualists. He has fastened the old house securely, and is now awaiting instructions from the society.

It is expected that prominent Spiritualists from all parts of the country will within the next few years hold a convention at Hydesville for the purpose of hearing Mr. Hyde's account of the discovery and to receive the bones.

The inhabitants of Hydesville thought that interest in the rappings had died with the Fox sisters, but with the find of Sunday, Spiritualist in this vicinity have already begun an agitation of their faith."

~~~

"Dr. John D. Quackenbos of Columbia, the authority on hypnotic suggestion and member of the Society for Psychical Research, said last night that he believed it was possible for a person through his subliminal self to become aware of the occurrence of something he had never personally seen or been informed of, as seemed to have been the case with Margaret (sic) Fox.

In the case of the Fox Sisters, Dr. Quakenbos said, I believe it was shown that their rappings were due to the snapping of their bones. I do not know what to think of this discovery of the skeleton in the cellar. It was possible, as has been demonstrated by our society's researchers for the Fox woman through psychical power to become aware of the murder and of the fact that the bones were hidden in the cellar.

Margaretta Fox, who called herself the widow of Dr. Kane, the Arctic explorer, once admitted to the writer that spirit rappings were a deception, and gave a convincing demonstration of her method of producing them by snapping the bones of her leg in and out of the ankle joint."

The Cottage & The Caretaker

The old cottage remained standing at the corner of Hydesville and Parker Road until it was moved to the Lily Dale Assembly in 1916 by the courtesy of Benjamin F. Bartlett of Pennsylvania. It was to become a shrine to the Fox Family and Modern Spiritualism. However, the cottage mysteriously burned to the ground in 1955.

A gentleman named John Drummond, who was a Spiritualist, had moved from Canada to Newark years before. He became an American citizen and worked as a newspaper correspondent and as a postal clerk. He was very fond of the cottage and its history. Tears came to his eyes that fateful day in 1916 when he watched the house roll down the street on a huge flatbed.

He just could not let it be. So he took it upon himself to rebuild a cottage of the exact size and room layout on the original foundation. When the construction was completed, John moved into the house and called himself "The Caretaker." John received no remuneration for his wonderful work. For some 60 years, he welcomed tourists and enjoyed telling them all about Spiritualism. He also had boxes full of literature that he had collected, freely handing out both pamphlets and news articles to any and all who would take them. John was in his glory promoting the Spiritualism he loved. All was well until the fateful day 40 years later when the house caught fire and partially burned once again. That didn't stop John. He purchased the materials and did what had to be done. He spent many happy days in the cottage until the next fateful day when the cottage succumbed to fire again. This time it would take more than John, now up in years, could handle.

However, he had determination. Since the cottage could not be rebuilt, John turned to the old school house on Parker Road. He decided to remodel the downstairs as a school house with rooms for classes and seminars. Living quarters and guest rooms were planned for the upstairs. Although he was well underway in making this effort a reality, the rebuilt school house was never completed. John was not well and although getting the best of care, John departed for the world of Spirit.

THE PROPERTY

On Thursday, December 4, 1947, the **Courier-Gazette** carried this article:

Fox Property Purchased by Society
Spiritualism Birthplace Here
Bought by Society for Shrine

"Hydesville, the crossroad birthplace of Modern Spiritualism, just north of Newark may soon be to Spiritualists what Cumorah Hill, south of Palmyra, is to the Mormons.

The site of the Fox cottage, where the famous mysterious rapping were heard by the Fox Sisters on March 31, 1848, was recently purchased by the Rev. J. Bertrand Gerling of the Universal Psychic Science Temple of Rochester in behalf of the Fox Memorial Society which has plans of erecting a shrine on the plot of ground.

The Fox Memorial Society was formed in January 1946 in Hudson, Ohio, by Mrs. Marian Sanford Pond, former Newark resident for the purpose of acquiring, maintaining and protecting the Hydesville site now so neglected, according to society officials. Mrs. Pond last July published her book, <u>Time is Kind—Unfortunate Story of the Fox Sisters,</u> a dramatized story of the origin of the cult.

With a membership of 300, the organization has its main purpose the perpetuation of the names of the founders of Modern Spiritualism, the three fox Sisters— Leah, Margaretta and Kate(sic)."

Although the property was recorded as having been deeded to the Fox Memorial, the Ministry of Spiritual and Divine Science, John Drummond in his Last Will & Testament, left the property to Janice & Roland Strassburger.

The severely burned cottage remained standing until it became a hazard to the community and was demolished by the Newark Fire Department in 1990.

In 1998, the National Spiritualist Association of Churches (NSAC) acquired the property. A committee was formed to plan the site as a Memorial Park to the memory of the Fox Sisters and the Hydesville rappings—"Mediums of the Advent of Modern Spiritualism." A structure was constructed upon the original rock foundation with windows all around the building. This allowed visitors to view the cellar walls of stone and the place where the peddler's body and trunk were found when the one wall caved in.

The NSAC has completed Phase I and II of the project. Hopefully the next step, Phase III, will be ongoing at the time of publication of this book. When completed the sign on the property shall read: "Hydesville Memorial Park." The marker placed by M. E. Cadwallader in December of 1927 will then find its way back to the property.

Today, the peddler's trunk,* paintings and pictures of the Fox Cottage, as well as a small replica of the house is on display in the Museum at the Lily Dale Assembly in Lily Dale, New York. From somewhere, a Holy Bible untouched by any of the fire has appeared with inscriptions (names) in its centerfold; however, they are not related to the Fox family. Recently some pictures of the Fox Family have been pasted in the inside cover for the visitor's

---

* Mr. William Duesler was first to ask the peddler if he carried a trunk. The Spirit rapped 'yes'. The contents had been removed by the murderer.

observation. It is inconceivable that the house having burned to the ground would allow only an unscathed Holy Bible to survive.

The news articles cleared the air once and for all. No matter what has been said in a derogatory manner about communication with those who have left their physical body and their soul having moved to a higher realm, it was dismissed by Maggie's "Recantation in 1889." And it was finally factually and totally dismissed by the finding of the peddler's skeleton and the peddler's trunk in the cellar of the dilapidated cottage that remained standing on the corner of Hydesville and Parker Road. Proof beyond a doubt was revealed by the finding of Rosna's skeleton by some children playing around the old house. The Fox children did in fact communicate with the peddler. Mrs. Fox had also communicated with the murdered peddler.

Think back a moment and recall it is March 31, 1848 and Katie just nine years old, snapping her fingers and having a response from the peddler. Then, Maggie, just 11 years old, calling out "Now, do as I do" counting "one, two, three, four" and asking the peddler to respond. The peddler responded with the same number of raps. Mrs. Fox continued the communication by asking many questions and the peddler rapped answering them correctly. He also answered correctly the questions asked by Mr. William Duesler and others. The Spirit revealed that he was a 31 year old man; had been murdered in the house for $500, his remains buried in the cellar, and his trunk emptied by the murderer. Communication with the peddler brought about the new age of Modern Spiritualism.

Leah – A Hero?

Just think—if it had not been for Leah Fox, all of this may have faded into the dust as it settled around Hydesville. All thanks be to Anna Leah Fox Underhill! She brought it to the world by starting with those early séances in her home in Rochester, New York. From there, in November 1849, the demonstration of mediumship was brought to the public at Corinthian Hall in Rochester. It was at that time that Spiritualism rapidly spread across the continent, across the ocean to Europe, and finally around the world.

That "light from beyond the tomb" has cast all doubt on the shadow that once existed. Spiritualism and communication with those who have left their physical bodies and whose souls have moved to a higher life termed the Spirit World are able to communicate with us at will. They are alive and well today!

XI
Fact & Fiction

Davenport's Inaccurate Claims

Section III of Reuben B. Davenport's book is entitled <u>History</u> and relates the story of the Fox family and the March 31, 1848 event at Hydesville. However, let's understand the difference between fact and fiction.

Fiction: Davenport stated that "Spiritualists 'pretend' that the so-called spirit rappings originated long before the Hydesville rappings. He claims this to be a wrong assertion."

> **FACT:** Spiritualism never made that pretension. Spiritualism has always differentiated between Ancient and Modern Spiritualism. If one researches Modern Spiritualism, it will be found that all phenomena before 1848 are considered Ancient Spiritualism.

Fiction: Davenport contends that the Fox sisters were the "first" of which there is an authentic account of rappings.

> **FACT:** This statement shows a lack of research since many centuries of phenomena had passed before the Hydesville event took place.

Fiction: Davenport states that Lizzie, Leah's daughter, was the fifth member of the Fox household in Hydesville in March 1848.

> **FACT:** Lizzie lived in Rochester with Leah. In May 1848, when they received the news of the events in Hydesville, Leah packed her suitcase and she and Lizzie traveled to Hydesville by way of the Erie Canal.

Fiction: Davenport states that Leah was 31 years old when the March 31st event took place.

> **FACT:** Leah was born in 1814. She was 34 at the time of March 31st event.

Fiction: Davenport states Katie exclaimed 'Mr. Splitfoot, do as I do.'

> **FACT:** Katie simply said 'Do as I do' according to the first book written in 1848 just after March 31st. It is entitled "A Report of the Mysterious Noises Heard in the House of Mr. John D. Fox in Hydesville, Arcadia, Wayne County; authenticated by the Certificates and confirmed by the Statements of the Citizens of that Place and Vicinity." It was Maggie that said, "Now do as I do.

Fiction: Davenport only acknowledged three children born in Rockland County.

> **FACT:** There were five children born in New City, Rockland County, N.Y.—namely Emily (1813), Anna Leah (1814), Maria (1816), Elizabeth (1818) and David (1820.

Fiction: Davenport records that Margaretta was born in 1840 and Catherine a year and a half later. That would make the girls ages six and eight at the time of the Hydesville event.

> **FACT:** Maggie was born on Saturday, October 7, 1837 and Katie was born on Wednesday, March 27, 1839—a difference of 18 months. Both were born in Consecon, Bath, Canada

Fiction: Davenport states March 31st was the 3rd night that the rappings occurred.

> **FACT:** Mrs. Fox tells us the noises began just after they moved into the house in December 1847. From March 15, 1848, the disturbances continued to build up until the night of March 31, 1848.

Fiction: Davenport states that in 1848 Katie went to Rochester to live with Leah; Maggie was not inclined to go.

> **FACT:** Many other records make it clear that Mr. Fox felt Katie, just nine years old, was too young to leave home. After a lot of convincing by Leah, Mr. Fox allowed Maggie to go with Leah and Lizzie to Rochester to live.

Fiction: Davenport says: "There is no doubt, too, that if there had not been a very strong vein of superstition in the Fox family, the first "rapping's" would never have been produced and... ."

> **FACT:** Mrs. Fox's family genealogy reveals a history of both mediums and psychics in the family and séances quite routine in their homes.

Davenport & Rochester

The Death-Blow to Spiritualism makes it very clear that Reuben Davenport in no way supported Spiritualism and was sure he could bring an end to it with facts or his use of fiction. Although Davenport uses every issue to prove his point, he also reveals the story of the events in the house in Rochester. Spirit activity was so strong that the whole family was frightened by it. Noises of all sorts prevailed and all sorts of things thrown across the room.

He records how Calvin's (Leah's second husband) bed was shaken, banged against the wall, as well as him having experienced several blows to the head. To add to Davenport's confusion, he relates Maggie's story, telling him she did all the same tricks in New York City. According to Greeley and others, this was not true.

Davenport goes on to malign the digging in the cellar of the Fox cottage, as well as the finding of human bones and hair in the first attempt to reveal the peddler's body as neighbors diligently dug in the cellar. It is clear he supports all investigators determined to find negative results. He not only attacks Spiritualism, but goes on to decry Hindu, Egyptian and any other beliefs which differed from his own.

Throughout his book, Davenport portrays Maggie as the predominant one in expressing her negativity toward Spiritualism and its phenomena. It is true that Maggie's husband, Dr. Kane, continuously begged her to stay away from the Spirits. However, through the bright days of her career as a medium, she was exuberant. There is no doubt that her involvement with Davenport, along with her problem with alcohol brought on her joyfully telling the untruths he wanted to hear.

Both Maggie and Katie labeled Leah Fox Underhill's book <u>The Missing Link in Modern Spiritualism</u> nothing but lies. It is true that there are inconsistencies found in the book; however most of the book falls in line with other writings of the that timeframe. Therefore, any researcher must go beyond Leah's book to determine fact from fiction. Some other issues to be considered:

Facts on Leah

Leah's book, <u>The Missing Link in Modern Spiritualism,</u> indicates she was widowed three times prior to reaching the age of 21. She could not have been widowed three times within that period of time. Her *first* marriage was to Bowman Fish in Rochester, N.Y., when she was just 14 and one-half years old. All stories relate that he deserted his wife and child. Her *second* marriage was to Calvin Brown on Wednesday, September 10, 1851; she would have been 37 years old based on her birth date of 1814. His death took place two years later. Her *third* marriage to Daniel Underhill took place on Tuesday, November 2, 1858 in Horace Greeley's home in New York City. Leah was now 44 years old. It appears the family was known to adjust their ages according to their need. Once Leah married Daniel, seven years her senior, she upped her age accordingly. During the 19th century, it often appears ages were casually changed to fit whatever the season of events.

Leah receives fury as well as praise. In the <u>Compendium</u> of <u>Modern Roman Law,</u> Henry D. Jencken, Katie's husband, writes "to the Fox family, Leah was seen as the witch who saw a way to make a lot of money; something she had never had and put the young girls into action for a lucrative livelihood. Leah and Calvin arranged for Maggie and Katie to go to many cities in upstate New York as well as N.Y. City……..and on to other states. Mrs. Fox was sent as a chaperone." While it is true, things did take place in this manner, let's look again.

On the other side of the coin, quoting the famed Spiritualist, Emma Floyd Hardinge Britten,

> "If ever Spiritualism proves a real and permanent blessing to mankind, the name of Ann Leah Fox Fish should stand conspicuous as one of the heroines of history who fought the battle against a world of opposition while her younger sisters were the only media and after she became so herself… ."

Another group of Spiritualists from Cincinnati Ohio, including Dr. Frank S. Bigelow, one of Andrew Jackson Davis' foster sons, gave Ann Leah an emblem to be worn on a chain that read: *A Tribute of Respect to Mrs. Ann L. Fish from Friends in Cleveland, 1851.* Leah also received a letter signed by eleven persons, including the designer of the medal that read

> "Dear Friend — We the undersigned present you with this emblem as a sincere token of our love and

affection. You have been faithful and steadfast in all your duties. You have been instrumental in bringing us to a realization of the truth of Immortality. May you be blessed with health and crowned with victory and triumph over your enemies, is the prayer of your united friends."

Maggie & Katie

In November of 1888, Maggie's curse of Spiritualism was recorded as well as her Music Hall address. She was quite pleased with herself. Katie was satisfied as well. And most of all, Reuben Davenport felt his job was very well done. Spiritualism was finally halted! He felt he had proudly revealed the death-blow to it. But time proved him wrong.

XII

Spiritualism's Stepping Stones
A Review

Mystery Solved One-By-One

Katie's support of Maggie's "Recantation" in 1888 should have cleared the air. After all, from 1848 up until their passing in the late 1800s, even through their years of severe alcoholism, they gave proof-positive evidence that the so-called dead do in fact return. They soothed many a grieving soul by giving irrefutable messages from deceased loved ones. The messages were facts that Maggie and Katie had no way of knowing, save for the voices from the great beyond. Maggie and Katie did prove beyond a shadow of doubt that those on the Spirit side of life could indeed contact their loved ones on earth plane. This communication proved that there is a continuity of life.

In Recognition

Mrs. Mary (Mercy) E. Cadwallader, owner and editor of the prestigious <u>Progressive Thinker</u> (1910-1934) and highly respected woman of Spiritualism, presented a plan at the International Spiritualist Congress in September 1925 to erect a monument in Rochester, New York, to commemorate the Birth of Modern Spiritualism. This idea was accepted with much enthusiasm. Provisions were made and in 1927, a stone obelisk was erected on the grounds of the Plymouth Spiritualist Church in Rochester adorned with a plaque stating: "Erected December 4, 1927 by the Spiritualists of the World in Commemoration of the Advent of Modern Spiritualism at Hydesville, N.Y., March 31, 1848." Some years later the church building was sold and the obelisk now stands in the City of Rochester near the point where Plymouth Avenue crosses Highway 490.

Mary E. Cadwallader also thought it necessary that some identification of the Advent of Modern Spiritualism should be made at the cottage of the Fox sisters in Hydesville. Therefore, she placed a stone marker in front of the cottage to the right of the front door that read:

**THE BIRTHPLACE OF
MODERN SPIRITUALISM
UPON THIS SITE STOOD THE HYDESVILLE
COTTAGE
THE HOME OF THE
FOX SISTERS
THROUGH WHOSE MEDIUMSHIP COMMUNICATION
WITH THE SPIRIT WORLD WAS ESTABLISHED
MARCH 31, 1848
THERE IS NO DEATH
THERE ARE NO DEAD**

PLACED HERE BY M.E. CADWALLADER
DEC. 5, 1927

After the NSAC purchased the Hydesville property in 1998, they initiated plans for Phase I of the Memorial Park. At that time, the project manager had the stone moved to the Mississippi Valley Spiritualist Camp in Iowa for safe keeping. At the conclusion of Phase III, the stone is to be returned to its home on the Fox property in Hydesville, N.Y.

Spiritualism's First Church

The famous Spiritualist pioneer, Warren B. Chase, said: "What Spiritualism needs is more dedicated, courageous, steadfast men daring to speak out and *Tell it Like it Is*." He led the way. In 1858, along with other noted pioneers, such as Cora Richmond and Dr. J. M. Peebles, the Harmonial Spiritualist Society was formed in Sturgis, Michigan. They erected the first Spiritualist Church in the United States. Today, only an inscribed rock remains identifying it and stating the property was donated to the city to be maintained as a free park.

Spiritualism Finally Organizes

Although for many years, the advocates of Modern Spiritualism had difficulty in their attempts to organize, it finally did happen. The first attempt in 1859 failed. They met again in Chicago in 1864 and tried again. At the same time, the First Spiritualist Society in Philadelphia, Pennsylvania, formed the first six principles of Modern Spiritualism. In 1865, the American Association of Spiritualists was founded and operated successfully until

1875. It has often been stated that it dissolved at that time because "the time was not right." Although in the 20th century this seemed to be a lame excuse, we can reflect on the past and understand it was no doubt true. The Victorian age was a difficult era for women.

Victoria Clafin Woodhull

Women and female mediums' input to an organization were not considered valid. Men basically ruled each Spiritualist group that made an attempt at organizing. This changed in 1875 when the notorious woman known for her youthful beauty, her flamboyant life style, her Wall Street Brokerage firm, as well as her mediumistic experiences, was invited to attend the Convention. The meeting proceeded—it all happened so fast. The votes were counted and Victoria Clafin Woodhull became the new President of the American Association of Spiritualists much to the surprise of all in attendance. She served for three years. At the time Victoria resigned, the organization was too damaged to be revived. Victoria was a Suffragist and well known for her famous speech for the National Women Suffrage Association. She was brilliant as well as a controversial figure and unfortunately although the women loved her in the Suffrage movement, they would not support her as the President of the American Association of Spiritualists. Without support of the women in the movement, she could do nothing but fail—and fail she did.

Five Great Leaders

Spiritualists did not attempt to organize again until five men from Washington, D.C., namely Henry Steinberg, O. W. Humphrey, Theodore J. Mayer, Maj. Robert Dimmick and Milan C. Edson, sent out subscriptions in 1892 for the organizing of a convention in Chicago, Illinois at the time of the World's Fair and the World Parliament of Religions (WPR). The idea was to set up an umbrella organization to unite all Spiritualists.

In September 1893 the convention met, founded The National Spiritualist Association—an umbrella that would include State Associations, churches, camps, and individuals. This was the root of the organization and these Spiritualists were true to their commitment to make Modern Spiritualism, founded by the Fox Sisters in Hydesville in 1848, the "Light of the World."

The Spiritualists intended to participate in the WPR and Cora L. V. Richmond, Spiritualism's famous orator, prepared her address on the Science, Philosophy and Religion of Spiritualism. However, the minutes of the WPR attendees list shows no Spiritualists in attendance and the program lists no Spiritualist orator. It is believed they were not invited since Spiritualism was not registered as a bonafide religion at that time.

Differences

The National Spiritualist Association (NSA) as an umbrella for all Spiritualists was productive. It set up the foundation from which all organizations could draw. Then in 1925, divisions came about due to different philosophies such as Reincarnation, Jesus, the Holy Bible, and race. Churches and groups began to relinquish their charters and once again became independently operated. Differences continued to rise and others continued to return their charters to the parent body. In 1953, the remnants of the NSA became The National Spiritualist Association of Churches. The organization continues to function in 2010 with a body of 80 churches and 12 active camps.

There are many various Spiritualist bodies active in the USA. Spiritualism is alive and well in the 21st Century.

Major Spiritualist Organizations USA - 2010

American Federation of Spiritualists, MA
American Spiritualist Association, FL
Atlanta Spiritualist Association, GA
Central N.Y. Spiritualist Association, NY
Federation of Spiritual Churches & Association CA
Fellowship of the Spirit, NY
Florida State Spiritualist Ministers Association, FL
General Assembly of Spiritualists, NY
Harmonial Philosophy Association, PA
Independent General Assembly, OH
Independent Spiritualist Association, MI
International General Assembly of Spiritualists, VA
Lily Dale Assembly, NY

National Spiritualist Alliance, MA
National Spiritualist Association of Churches, NY
Universal Harmony Foundation, FL
Universal Spiritualists Association, IN

Spiritualist Camps Active in 2010:

Camp Edgewood, WA
Camp Etna, ME
Chain Lake Spiritualist Camp, MI
Cherry Valley Spiritualist Camp, IL
Chesterfield Spiritualist Camp, IN
Harmony Grove, CA
Ladies Aid Society Incorporated, CT
Lily Dale Assembly, NY
Madison Spiritualist Camp, ME
Mississippi Valley Spiritualist Association Camp, IA
Northern Lake Michigan Spiritualist Camp, MI
On-I-Set Wigwam, MA
Snowflake Spiritualist Camp, MI
Southern Cassadaga Spiritualist Campmeeting Association, FL
Sun Spiritualist Camp, AZ
Sunset Spiritualist Camp, KS
Temple Heights, ME
Western Wisconsin Spiritualist Camp Association, WI

Spiritualist Schools in 2010:

Harmony Grove Institute, CA
Holistic Studies, Inc., NY
IGAS Healing & Learning Center, OH
Morris Pratt Institute, WI
Universal Institute of Holistic Study, IN

Since Spiritualists and churches are found all over the world without a central focal point, there is no procedure today for tracking the number of Spiritualists or churches today, it can only be estimated from available sources. It appears the total number of Spiritualists in the world may be just under 200,000. It is also noted that in today's climate, a very large number of people are seeking spirituality outside of the church and may knowingly or unknowingly practice the beliefs of Spiritualism.

Spiritualism's Motto

As the Sunflower turns its face to the Light of the Sun, Let Spiritualism turn the face of Humanity to the Light of Truth!

XIII
Conclusion

No Defense Needed

Spiritualism did not ever need to be defended nor does it need to be defended now. Truth has always been and always will be. In no way is this book a defense of Spiritualism or its phenomena. The purpose of this book is solely to bring forth the facts and clarify sections of Reuben Briggs Davenport's book The Death-Blow to Spiritualism written and published by G. W. Dillingham in 1888.

Although it is obvious that Davenport was delighted in his attempt to denounce Spiritualism and bring a death-blow to it, it became outstandingly clear in 1889, that it did not happen. In addition, finding the peddler's skeleton and his trunk in 1904 only further clarified Spiritualism was alive and well. Davenport was not successful in his attempt.

Steps in Killing The Death-Blow

To restate the facts and keep the record straight: The first positive step in killing Reuben Briggs Davenport's The Death-Blow to Spiritualism took place in November 1889 when Maggie Fox Kane made her famous "Recantation." That was just one year after she offered her Curse of Spiritualism. She had to recant! She had no other choice!

Why? Simply because she knew full well that in March 1848, she had clearly communicated with the unseen peddler. She knew she had communicated with the unseen world of Spirit from 1848 until this very moment. The very fact that she had told a "horrible untruth' bothered her conscience. It was causing her great discomfort. It is clear that in 1888, she had not told the truth when she denied the facts of her communication with the World of Spirit.

The second positive step in killing Davenport's theory was the incident reported in several newspapers in 1904 when the wall of the cellar of the cottage at Hydesville collapsed and revealed the peddler's skeleton and his trunk.

These two events provided the factual additional proof — "evidence beyond a shadow of a doubt"—that it indeed was Charles B. Rosna who first communicated with Katie, Maggie, Mrs. Fox, and many of the neighbors on March 31, 1848 and thereafter. Both of these actions finally killed Davenport's death-blow.

Founders of Modern Spiritualism

The documents bearing the facts are presented here for all to read and digest for themselves. It is quite evident that it is appropriate to label Margaretta Fox Kane and Catherine Fox Jencken the "Founders of Modern Spiritualism." However, we must always remember that without the role played by Leah Fox Fish-Brown-Underhill, her two young sisters and the happenings of March 31, 1848, might have faded away forever to be forgotten.

Conclusion

It is recorded in The Spiritualist written by Ruth Brandon that "Leah Fish sensed the financial as well as religious opportunities which were made available to her from the sensation offered by Margaret's (sic) demonstrations. And, the dual prospect of financial gain and the excitement of creating a new cult fascinated Leah. She made the most of both by dominating the other members of the family through fear and coercion."

But on the other side of the coin, the famous Spiritualist, Emma Hardinge Britten wrote to the Spiritualists,

> "Leah Ann (sic) is one of the heroines of history who fought the battle against a world of opposition while her younger sisters were the only media and after she herself became... ." My opinion, all three were heroines of history who fought... ."

Yet another, in his book A Plea for Preservation of all the Facts Concerning the Early Manifestations of the Most Comprehensive Philosophy of Life, published in the Progressive Thinker in 1890 Ben F. Hayden declared:

> "It seems to me to be a fitting time for us to question ourselves as to whether we are, or have been, doing all that we can do to preserve all the facts concerning the early manifestations of the most comprehensive philosophy of life that has ever been known among mankind. This year we celebrated the sixty-second* anniversary. Certainly, we as, believers of Truth, observed its yearly return with appropriate ceremonies; congratulating

---

* The Year 1890

ourselves and rejoicing with our arisen ones because the veil has been rended and we can and do know of the whence and the whither of our so-called dead.

Every Spiritualist knows of the Fox sisters. Their names and fame have gone throughout the civilized world as the first interpreters of the Hydesville rappings, converting the hitherto unintelligible sounds at an ordinary haunted house the most stupendous discovery of any age since time began, which fully answers the every-recurring question, 'If a man die, shall he live again?'

Wherever Spiritualism is known, their (sic) merited praises have been sung and their names revered. This is as it should be, and I would be the last to pluck a single laurel from the immortal wreath of their world-wide fame. Not only would I pronounce the most extravagant laudations in honor of the angel-blessed sisters, but I would fain extend the need of praise to every other medium throughout the world that courageously and conscientiously stands as an open gateway between the two realms of existence, giving to us a true knowledge of conditions met within that higher life.

While we are perfectly familiar with the names of Margaretta and Catherine Fox, how many of us are as familiar with the name of Charles B. Rosna, the poor murdered peddler, whose physical life was snuffed out, and his body buried in the cellar of the Hydesville Cottage? Charles B. Rosna, the defleshed immortal Spirit, stood on the invisible side of life and gave to these girls the knowledge that he, though destroyed in the physical still survived in the Spirit;

that knowledge is so full of blessings for all the human race which is destined to banish all skepticism and infidelity from the minds of men; comforting the mourner with angelic consolations; lifting the unfortunate and the outcast, the inebriate and taking away the sting of death which has kept mankind under the bondage through fear, so that now death to its millions of believers is but the kind and gentle servant 'who unlocks with noiseless hand life's flower encircled door, to show us those we loved.'

What a wondrous debt of gratitude do we owe to this poor itinerant salesman, Charles B. Rosna. I would wrest his name from that obscurity into which it has been permitted to lapse and place it among those of the greatest benefactors of the human race; and, like the name of Abou Ben Adhem of old, I would have it 'lead all the rest.' Truly, Charles B. Rosna brought 'life and immortality to light' in an age when it was most supremely needed. His name should be nailed to the masthead of every paper published in the interest of the cause which he represents.

I would that his name and accomplished mission were inscribed in golden letters upon the title page of every book and pamphlet issued from the spiritual press. It should adorn the walls of every Spiritualist Church and be framed as a motto and hung in every Spiritualist home throughout the world. In short, among Spiritualists, at least, I would have the name of Rosna as familiar as that of Jesus among Christians. I would have the name of Charles B. Rosna so closely blended with that of the Fox sisters that one would not be spoken without thinking of the other, and while the

Christian minister is performing the last rites and ceremonies over the bier of the departed, telling the mourners he has gone to that bourne from which no traveler ever returns, I would have all remember that Charles B. Rosna proclaimed to the world that the dead do return and stand ready awaiting for an invitation and opportunity to declare that we still live and for a purpose; and as we live so shall ye live also. Therefore, Margaretta and Catherine Fox and Charles B. Rosna, now, henceforth and forever."

Davenport's <u>The Death-Blow to Spiritualism</u> failed miserably. It did not kill Spiritualism. Spiritualism is alive and well in the 21st Century.

The light from beyond the tomb forever flashes brightly and directly on the names of:

$$\left\{ \begin{array}{c} \text{CHARLES B. ROSNA – THE PEDDLER} \\ \text{LEAH FOX UNDERHILL} \\ \text{MARGARETTA FOX KANE} \\ \text{CATHERINE FOX JENCKEN} \end{array} \right\}$$

The End

Appendix A - Participants

Members of the Fox Family's

Fox-Jencken, Catherine	aka Kate or Katie
Jencken, Henry Diedrich	Kate's husband
Jencken, Ferdinand L.D.	Kate's son
Fish, Elizabeth	aka Lizzie; Leah's daughter
Fox-Fish-Brown-Underhill, Leah	Anna Leah (given name), aka A. Leah, or Ann
Fox-Kane, Margaretta	aka Maggie or Margaret
Fox, Mrs. Margaret	Mother
Fox, Mr. John David	Father
Fox, David Stephen Fox	Brother
Fox, Elizabeth Culver	David's wife
Kane, Dr. Elisha Kent	Maggie's husband
Underhill, Daniel	Leah's husband

Others

Bell Family	Rented the cottage 1843-4
Bigelow, Dr. Frank S.	Foster son of A.J. Davis
Britten, Emma Hardinge	Spiritualist
Cadwallader, M. E.	Owner The Progressive Thinker
De Barr. Mme. Diss	Medium
Chase, Warren B.	Famous Pioneer of Spiritualism
Drummond, John	Caretaker of the Cottage
Duesler, William & Wife	Neighbors in Hydesville
Eliab W. Capron	Friend of Leah
Franklin, Sir John	Arctic Explorer
Greeley, Horace	Editor/Owner New York Times

Hyde, Dr. Henry .... Original owner of the cottage
Hyde, Artemas W. .... Dr. Hyde's son
Keeler, P.L.O.A. .... Medium
Laud, Maud .... Medium
Lieper, Mrs. .... Kane's aunt
Mason .... Congressional office
Newton, Mr. Henry J .... Spiritualist
Peebles, Dr. James M. .... Pioneer of Spiritualism
Pulver Lucretia .... Housekeeper for the Bell family
Quackenbos, Dr. John D .... Society for Psychical Research
Pond, Marian Sanford............... Daughter-in-law of David Fox
Post, Amy & Isaac..................... Hicksite Quakers, befriended
Redfield, Mr . & Mrs. .... Neighbors in Hydesville
Richmond, Cora L. V. .... Noted Orator of Spiritualism
Rosna, Charles B .... Murdered Peddler
Seybert, Henry .... Philanthropist
Shields, James .... Senator – Illinois
Slade, Henry .... Medium
Tallmadge, Nathanial................ Gov. Wisconsin & Senator
Weekman, Michael & Family ... Renters of the cottage 1846-7
Weller .... Congressional office
Wells, Mrs. .... Medium
Willets, Mr. . ... Friend of Capron

Appendix B - Directions to Hydesville Memorial Park

The Fox Cottage
1510 Hydesville Road, Hydesville

From Lily Dale, New York

I-90 in Fredonia
Stay on I-90 East to Exit 43
.... toward Palmyra (toll) Exit 31
Turn right to Newark on Rte. 88
Cross the Erie Canal
Left turn past Granite Works
Stay on 88 to Hydesville Road
Turn on to Hydesville Road
....Pass Cemetery on Main Street to
1510 Hydesville Road
On Corner of Hydesville Road & Parker Ave.

From Albany, New York

West on I-90
To Exit 31, Palmyra
Turn right to Newark on Rte. 88
Cross the Erie Canal
Pass the Granite Works
Stay on Rte. 88 to Hydesville Road
Turn on to Hydesville Road
Pass Cemetery on Main Street to
1510 Hydesville Road situated on
Corner of Hydesville Rd. & Parker Ave.

Reference Material

Annals of Psychical Science ..... Issue: June 1905
Britten, Emma Hardinge .... Modern American Spiritualism, 1870
Brown, Slater .... The Heyday of Spiritualism, 1970
Cadwallader, M. E. .... Hydesville in History, 1917
Capron, E. W. .... Modern Spiritualism, 1855
Davenport, Reuben B .... The Death-Blow to Spiritualism, 1888
Edmonds, I. G. .... The Girls who Spoke to Ghosts, 1979
Edmonds, J. W. .... Spiritualism (2 Vol) 1852 & 1855
Fodor, Nandor .... Encyclopedia of Psychic Science, 1966
Fornell, Earle W .... The Unhappy Medium, 1964
Jackson, Herbert G. Jr .... The Spirit Rappers, 1972
Kane, Maggie Fox .... Love Life of Dr. Kane, 1865
King-Hall, Magdalen .... The Fox Sisters, 1950
Lewis, E.E. .... A Report of the Mysterious Noises Heard in the House of Mr. John Fox in Hydesville, Arcadia, Wayne County; authenticated by the Certificates and confirmed by the Statements of the Citizens of that Place and Vicinity, 1848
Owen, Robert Dale .... The Debatable Land between This World and the Next, 1871
Owen, Robert Dale .... Footfalls on the Boundaries of Another World, 1860
Pond, Mariam Buckner .... Time is Kind, 1947
Somerlott, Robert .... Here, Mr. Splitfoot, 1971

Stuart, Nancy Rubin .... The Reluctant Spiritualist, 2005
Taylor, Wm. G. .... Katie Fox & the Taylor Records (old)
Underhill, A. Leah Fox .... The Missing Link, 1855

Other

Seybert .... Commission Report: 1883-1887, 1920
Boston News Journal .... November 23, 1904
Rochester Democrat .... November 22, 1904
Rochester Democrat .... November 23, 1904

About the Author

Marilyn J. Awtry has been a researcher in the field of Spiritualism for over forty years. This has credited her with the title of "The Encyclopedia of Spiritualism of the 20th Century." She is well-known as an orator, teacher, and author having 27 publications to her credit. She is a columnist for a monthly newspaper titled <u>The Psychic World</u> out of England as well as <u>The National Spiritualist Summit</u>. She has been a featured columnist in several secular and spiritual magazines.

For three years, Marilyn served as Editor of <u>Speakout,</u> a monthly publication of The Harmonial Philosophy Association. She also was owner and Editor of a monthly paper <u>The Cassadagan.</u>

She has been listed in <u>Who's Who of American Women</u> and <u>Who's Who of Women of the World.</u> The <u>National Geographic Traveler's Magazine</u> featured a full-page article about her varied endeavors. Marilyn was featured on the Maury Povich TV Show—a story about the Southern Cassadaga Spiritualist Association in Florida.

In this present release, she has authored and compiled a book that brings to light the facts of 1889 and 1904 that completely changed the story that had been written in 1888. It gives substance to the fact that Spiritualism is alive and well in the 21st Century.

Author's Publications

River of Life – How to Live in the Flow
Provides an outline of 72 of the Spiritual Natural Laws as well as selected physical laws. A self-help to unfoldment is provided in the back pages of the book.

Philosophy of Spiritualism for the 21st Century
An outline of definitions relating to Philosophy, Natural Law, Spiritualism's basic teachings, the Universe, the Earth, the Spirit World and more.

You and a Way
A guide for the seeker of truth.

Spiritualism's Understanding of The Holy Bible
Guide to understanding how Spiritualism reflects on the teachings of the Holy Bible.

They Paved the Way (Spiritualism's Pioneers)
A brief on the pioneers of the movement. A new three volume series now in the making. Vol I – Pioneers 1848-1898, Vol II - The Torchbearers 1899-1949, Vol III - The Workers in the Vineyard from 1950 to Present in the USA & Around the World.

Souvenir: Spiritualism's Millennium Calendar
Historical data entered day-by-day from 1810-2000.

LaVergne, TN USA
23 September 2010
198170LV00001BA/1/P